A
GLIMPSE
OF
JESUS

❧

A GLIMPSE OF JESUS

The Stranger to Self-Hatred

❧

BRENNAN MANNING

HarperSanFrancisco
A Division of HarperCollins*Publishers*

FIRST EDITION
Designed by Joseph Rutt

Library of Congress Cataloging-in-Publication Data
Manning, Brennan.
A glimpse of Jesus : the stranger to self-hatred / Brennan Manning.
p. cm.
Includes bibliographical references.
ISBN 0–06–000069–4 (cloth)
1. Self-acceptance—Religious aspects—Christianity.
2. Christian life. I. Title.
BV4647.S43 M36   2002
248.4—dc21   2002032808

03 04 05 06 07 RRD(H) 10 9 8 7 6 5 4 3 2 1

For Jack and Jan Carter, who demolished the myth that you can't be cool and Christian, whose unique Southern Baptist thinking is more catholic than mine, and whose hearts are like a bloodshot sunset.

TABLE OF CONTENTS

FOREWORD

This little book pretends to be no more than the title claims: a glimpse of Jesus. That is all I have. It was written for myself and anyone else who has been tyrannized by self-hatred. I envision a wide reading audience, because self-hatred is the predominant spiritual problem that I've had to deal with in twenty-eight years as a vagabond evangelist.

Unhealthy guilt, shame, remorse, and self-hatred are no respecters of persons. Vague feelings of existential uneasiness before the Lord God transcend poverty and wealth, cultural and educational differences, distinctions between clergy and laity.

While *A Glimpse of Jesus* is polemical in places, and questions the vision of certain authority figures in the church, it never questions the personal integrity or the pastoral concern of their ministries. Blaming the church is a jejune, counterproductive defense mechanism for which I have neither the time nor the heart. The church has been and will remain the locus of my encounter with Jesus Christ. One of the several purposes within these pages is to contribute to the raising of community consciousness at the grassroots level. A fearless reexamination of pastoral values, attitudes, and practices is part of the ongoing task of perennial reform.

The sweeping implications of the social dimension of the gospel, so vital for Christian renewal, are left largely untreated here because of the limited scope of the subject. A glimpse is a glimpse and nothing more. And nothing less either.

Perhaps what is decisive is not how much we see, but how much we trust and follow Jesus of Nazareth, however sketchy the portrait, however partial the glimpse.

ACKNOWLEDGMENTS

The insights of many Christian writers, teachers, and friends are so integral to this book that, except for a few personal experiences, the true author is the Body of Christ.

My publisher, Stephen Hanselman, insists that I am a better writer than I really am. Without his encouragement, this book would not have seen the light of day. My heartfelt gratitude to my office manager, Ann Walker, who used her considerable gifts so generously, thus allowing me time to write. And to Paul Sheldon, Gene and Carol Barnes, Ed and Hillary Moise, close friends all, who drag me out to dinner and a movie when I forget to balance work with play. And to my literary agent, Kathy Helmers, whose probing critique enriches every book I write. Alas, my gratitude to the readers who write and encourage me to keep on writing, even when I feel that I have nothing more to say.

A
GLIMPSE
OF
JESUS

❧

THE SCRIPT FOR SELF-HATRED

Repetitio est mater studiorum, goes the old Latin proverb. Since repetition is the mother of study, I begin this book with a story previously cited in my 1994 work, *Abba's Child*.

If repression was the predominant defense mechanism of the past century, projection takes pride of place today. And so we turn to Flannery O'Connor's short story "The Turkey."[1] The anti-hero and principal protagonist is a little boy named Ruller. He has a poor self-image because nothing he turns his hand to ever seems to work.

One night in bed Ruller overhears his parents analyzing him. "Ruller's an unusual one," his father says. "Why does he always play by himself?" His mother answers, "How am I to know?"

One day in the woods Ruller spots a wild and wounded turkey and sets off in hot pursuit. "Oh, if only I can catch it," he cries. He *will* catch it, even if he has to run it out of state. He sees himself triumphantly marching through the front door of his house with the turkey slung over his shoulder and the whole family screaming, "Look at Ruller with that wild turkey! Ruller, where did you get that turkey?"

"Oh, I caught it in the woods. Maybe you would like me to catch you one sometime."

But then a troubling thought flashes across his mind: "God will probably make me chase that damn turkey all afternoon for nothing." Hmmn, shouldn't think that way about God though; yet that was the way he felt. If that was the way he felt, could he help it? He wondered if he was unusual.

Ruller finally captures the turkey when it rolls over dead from a previous gunshot wound. He hoists it on his shoulders and begins his messianic march back through the center of town. He remembers the things he had thought before he got the bird. They were pretty bad, he guesses. He figures God had stopped him before it was too late. He should be very thankful.

"Thank you, God," he says. "Much obliged to you. This turkey must weigh ten pounds. You were mighty generous."

Maybe getting the turkey was a sign, he thinks. Maybe God wanted him to be a preacher. He thinks of Bing Crosby and Spencer Tracy.

Ruller enters town with the turkey slung over his shoulder. He wants to do something for God, but he doesn't know what to do. If anybody was playing the accordion on the street today, he would give that musician his dime. It was the only dime he had, but he would give it to them anyway.

Two men approach and whistle at the turkey. They yell at some other men on the corner to look. "How much do you think it weighs?" they ask.

"At least ten pounds," Ruller answers.

"How long did you chase it?"

"About an hour," says Ruller.

"That's really amazing. You must be very tired."

"No, but I have to go," Ruller replies. "I'm in a hurry." He can't wait to get home.

He begins to wish that he would see somebody begging. Suddenly he prays, "Lord, send me a beggar. Send me one before I get home." God had put the turkey there. Surely God will send him a beggar. He knows for a *fact* that God will send him one. God is interested in him because he is an unusual child.

"Please, one right now"—and the minute he says it, an old beggar woman heads straight at him. His heart is stomping up and down in his chest. As they near each other, Ruller springs at the woman, shouting, "Here, here," thrusts the dime into her hand, and dashes on without looking back.

Slowly his heart calms and he begins to feel full of a new feeling—like being happy and embarrassed at the same time. Maybe, he thinks, he will give all his money to her. He feels as if the ground doesn't need to be under him any longer.

Ruller notices a group of country boys shuffling behind him. He turns round and asks generously, "Y'all wanna see this turkey?"

They stare at him. "Where did ya git that turkey?"

"I found it in the woods. I chased it dead. See, it's been shot under the wing."

"Lemme see it," one boy says. Ruller hands him the turkey. The turkey's head flies into Ruller's face as the country boy

3

slings it up in the air and over his own shoulder and turns. The others turn with him and saunter away.

They are a quarter-mile away before Ruller moves. Finally he realizes that he can't even see the boys anymore, they were so far away. Then he turns toward home, almost creeping.

He walks for a bit and then, noticing it is dark, suddenly begins to run. O'Connor's exquisite tale ends with the words: "He ran faster and faster, and as he turned up the road to his house, his heart was running as fast as his legs and he was certain that Something Awful was tearing behind him with its arms rigid and its fingers ready to clutch."[2]

The story hardly needs any commentary, for in little Ruller many of us Christians stand revealed, naked, exposed. Our God is the One who benevolently gives turkeys and then capriciously takes them away. When he gives them, they are a sign of his interest, favor, and good pleasure with us. We feel comfortably close to God and are spurred to the heights of generosity. When he takes them away, it is a sign of his displeasure, rejection, and vengeance. We feel cast off by God. He is fickle, unpredictable, and whimsical. He builds us up only to let us down. He relentlessly remembers our past sins and vindictively retaliates by snatching the turkeys of good health, wealth, inner peace, empire, success, and joy.

PROJECTIONISM

The script for self-hatred starts with this distorted view of God. As mathematician/philosopher Blaise Pascal wrote,

"God made man in his own image and man returned the compliment."[3] The mechanism of projection is a process of unwittingly ascribing to God our own attitudes and feelings as an unconscious defense of our own inadequacy or guilt.

"Indeed," notes writer James Burtchaell,

> much of the distortion that does enter into our notion of God is introduced in each person's formative period—his youth. From his parents a child learns of a God who strongly disapproves of disobedience, and hitting one's brothers and sisters and telling lies. The youngster goes to school and finds that God also shares the many concerns, sometimes fussy ones, of his teachers. At church, the pastor's God has a somewhat different set of priorities. First and foremost is the urgency of "growing the church," quadrupling the membership in three years. Though it is beyond his own horizon of interest, the child is aware that God often makes recurring and emphatic fiscal demands upon the people. When he reaches the age for high school, he finds that God's own interests have expanded: he is obsessed with sex and drinking and drugs.[4]

Eventually, observes Burtchaell, the maturing young person draws a disturbing conclusion from God's shifting interests:

> After he emerges from his youth altogether he discovers—sometimes with resentment—that God has been used as a sanction for all those who were responsible for

his discipline. When he used to cavort a bit mischievously at home, his mother might reach the end of her patience and persuasiveness and threaten, "When Daddy comes home, he'll take care of you." But if Mommy and Daddy are both at their wits' end, there is always the eternal spanking to which they can and do allude. God is thus unwittingly associated with fear.[5]

The Christian world, which incessantly projects its own god fashioned after its own image, pays a heavy price in anxiety, a scrupulosity that sees sin where there is no sin, and a vague sense of existential guilt. As Jesuit Bernard Bush notes,

These feelings come from within ourselves and are projected outward into the mind of God. We may find that we punish ourselves mercilessly for real or imagined sins, and even then we will not forgive ourselves. . . . Fortunately Christ has revealed the real God to us in unmistakably human form, exposed projection for the idolatry that it is, and given us the way to become free from it. It takes a profound conversion to accept the belief that God is tender and loves us just as we are, not in spite of our sins and faults, but with them. God does not condone or sanction evil, but he does not withhold his love because there is evil in us. The key to this understanding is the way we feel about ourselves. We cannot even stand or accept love from another human being when we do not love ourselves, much less believe or accept that God could possibly love us.[6]

Whether envisioned as an omnipotent thug stealing our inner peace or as Something Awful tearing behind us, these distortions and caricatures of the God revealed by and in Jesus engender fear, anger, self-hatred, and a nagging sense of insecurity about ever being in right relationship with God. As I've tramped about the country as an evangelist over the years, dealing with a cross section of humanity from CEOs to street people, it has become luminously clear that religious projection is remarkably widespread and that self-hatred is rampant.

PERFECTIONISM

The perfectionist in the spiritual life is locked into the saint-or-sinner syndrome, tyrannized by an all-or-nothing mentality. Informed by his spiritual director that he is probably in the sixth mansion of St. Teresa's *Interior Castle*, the perfectionist grieves that he is not in the seventh. He vows to try harder and searches the library to see if Richard Foster, Tilden Edwards, or Gerald May have written anything new on mysticism. Compulsive and constant moralistic self-evaluation precludes the serene acceptance of his poverty before God.

"I hope it is clear that feelings of guilt, accompanied by anxiety, fear and restlessness, arise from deep within ourselves and are not an accurate gauge of the state of our souls before God," cautions Bernard Bush. "We cannot assume that he feels about us the way we feel about ourselves, unless we love ourselves intensely and freely."[7]

7

The perfectionist interprets weakness as mediocrity and inconsistency as a loss of nerve. Their desire for perfection is so acute that it transcends the desire for God. The witness of Mother Teresa, Rosa Parks, Billy Graham, and Tony Campolo is received not as an inspiration but as a reproach. The painful consciousness of having sold out for small comforts that now seem indispensable and small compromises (growing ever more numerous) that now seem irreversible is a source of deep distress.

A compassionate attitude of self-acceptance is simply unacceptable to the perfectionist. The notions that sin and grace can coexist simultaneously in the same person and that imperfection and inspiration are not mutually exclusive are maudlin concessions valid only for those not striving for spiritual excellence. Yet St. Paul writes, "Though the will to do what is good is in me, the performance is not, with the result that instead of doing the good things I want to do, I carry out the sinful things I do not want" (Rom. 7:18–19). Bush notes, of this common human failing, "It has never been expressed so succinctly. St. Paul can even find the hand of God and a response of praise in the contemplation of his own sinfulness."[8]

But because the perfectionist measures her personal worth before God in terms of the acquisition of virtue and the elimination of vice, because her vision is a triumphal forced march along the purgative and illuminative trails to the unitive bivouac, the outcome is an unrealistically negative self-image. There's a conspicuous absence of peace and joy. The yawning gulf between the ideal self and the real self makes an attitude of gratitude impossible and the likelihood of wide mood swings highly probable.

"Perfectionist individuals, we find, are likely to respond to the perception of failure or inadequacy with a precipitous loss in self-esteem that can trigger episodes of severe depression and anxiety."[9] Even the compulsive drive for *spiritual* perfection, born not of the Spirit of God but of the needs of this world, only adds another scenario to the script for self-hatred.

MORALISM/LEGALISM

The habit of moralizing spoils religion. Personal responsibility to an inviolable moral code replaces personal response to God's loving call. Moralism and its stepchild, legalism, reduce the love story of God for his people to the observance of burdensome duties and oppressive laws. The legalist deformation of religion concerns itself with shadow, not substance.

At the funeral home, a well-intentioned friend eulogized the deceased: "John was a wonderful Christian. He never missed church, was married only once, and never told a dirty joke." Here the criterion for holiness and the ultimate sign of religious surrender is observance of the law. The Pharisees did as much!

Legalism creates a mask of conformity which makes the believer holy in his eyes and thus prevents him from coming to self-knowledge. Legalistic religion stresses will-power, and it is this very stress on personal effort that makes the legalist unaware of his real feelings, of his own brokenness, and hence of his need for redemption. . . . He tends to despise the men and women who are not as observant as he. Thus he elevates himself above the sinner, the outsider, the non-conformist. Because of this self-elevation, this reliance on self, coupled with lack of self-knowledge, the legalist renders himself incapable of receiving divine grace; he does not live by faith.[10]

Recent history attests that the Moral Majority in the United States represented a pathetic caricature of biblical religion. The face of a compassionate God was completely obscured; the best principles of the Christian heritage were ignored in favor of a hard moralism, wherein the demonic dimension overshadowed the loving dimension of the gospel. Their legalistic formulations attempted to dominate American moral perspective, limit moral options, and even replace moral insight. The god of the Moral Majority was an exacting lawgiver, a stern taskmaster; the Good News of Jesus Christ took on a cutting fanatical edge; the force of the gospel message was distorted into something basically threatening.

"The smug Christian finds a perverse vindictive satisfaction in anticipating the fate of those whom he considers his own enemies and God's as well," notes ethicist James Gaffney:

Thus certain elements present in the New Testament can be isolated and inflated to a point where they distort the whole central significance of the New Testament and pervert the whole character of the Christian life. Just as Christian belief has its heresies of thought, so too Christian ethics has its heresies of attitude and behavior. To accept the Gospel in faith is to respect its emphases and preserve its balance.[11]

Let the Christian community cry out in anger against the lying moralistic slogans that pile up with impunity! Reverend Jerry Falwell decried the horror of pornography yet justified the proliferation of nuclear weapons and the use of the atomic bomb! (It sounded rational: a bit of genocide is a minor evangelical matter compared to getting the smut-peddlers off the street.) Approximately 350 years ago Blaise Pascal wrote prophetically, "Men never do evil so completely and cheerfully as when they do it from religious convictions."[12]

On national TV, Pat Robertson, nodding like a metronome, emboldened Falwell, as the latter blamed 9/11/01 on gays, feminists, abortionists, People of the American Way, and the ACLU—for provoking the murderous wrath of God. Falwell's gimlet-eyed god resembles himself, a deity of appetite and fanaticism, who calmly issues a summons to *jihad*. What a travesty of the gospel and what bad press for authentic religion! "The creator whom one can play off against the creature is a false god," writes biblical scholar Ernst Käsemann, "and false gods rob even pious people of their humanity, as is shown times without number in the church's history."[13]

Unfortunately, religion readily lends itself to legalistic misunderstanding. A reliance on ceremonies and the observance of commandments too easily leads to a false trust in the external elements of religion and creates a mystique of spiritual superiority. Does the neutral onlooker identify a Christian by his pious practices and cultic regularity or by the loving quality of his everyday presence in the workaday world? "The greatest millstone around the neck of organized religion," claims author Barbara Doherty, "is not its authority figures but the too facile acceptance on the part of leaders and members that ritual and cult can substitute for personal commitment and the sacrifice of one's life."[14]

From another perspective, legalism attempts to determine every moral choice on the basis of existing regulations. Law thus tends to become an end in itself rather than a means to an end. The result is the frustration of the very motive that brought religious law into being. Jesus resolutely insisted that law was the expression of the love of God and neighbor and that piety that stands in the way of love stands in the way of God himself. "Such freedom challenged the Jewish system," notes New Testament scholar John O'Grady. "Yet Jesus says he has not come to destroy the law but to fulfill it. What he offers is not a new law but a new attitude toward law, an attitude based on being human and loving."[15]

Furthermore, Jesus shattered the legalistic notion of reward for moral performance and the arrogant expectation of a higher rung on the heavenly ladder. The bartering mentality of "I've done this; therefore, you owe me that" is brushed aside in the scandalous parable of the laborers in the vineyard (Matt. 20:1–16). Salvation cannot be earned or merited but only humbly and gratefully received as a loving gift from the Father's hand.

In Flannery O'Connor's short story "Revelation," Mrs. Turpin is a perverse, self-righteous Christian woman who despises blacks (whom she calls *niggers*), white trash, the physically impaired (whom she calls *freaks*), and the mentally challenged (whom she calls *lunatics*). Standing in front of the pigpen in her backyard, she has a vision—the "revelation." From the ground, a brilliant, swinging, fiery bridge is raised from earth to heaven, and along that bridge "a vast horde of souls were rumbling toward heaven. There were whole companies of white trash, clean for the first time in their lives, and battalions of black niggers in white robes and battalions of freaks and lunatics shouting and clapping and leaping like frogs, and finally a whole tribe of people just like herself marching behind the others with great dignity, accountable as they had always been for good order and common sense and respectable behavior. They alone were on key. Yet she could see by their shocked and altered faces that even their virtues were being burned away."[16]

All is gift and gracious clemency, as the parable of the prodigal son vividly reminds us. Dutch theologian Edward Schillebeeckx writes,

> To demand a higher reward for achievement (because, for instance, one lives a celibate life for the kingdom's sake) and to become angry (because the younger brother, who likewise has offered his life for the cause of

the kingdom, gets married) is by this parable held up to ridicule as an attitude directly militating against the praxis of the kingdom of God. Whatever the material verdict on the case, both celibacy as being a claim upon a higher reward and being resentful of the younger brother are attitudes alien to the *orthopraxis* of the kingdom of God.[17]

The sex scandal that continues to roil the Roman Catholic Church is a tragedy of horrific proportions, not only because the despicable actions of a tiny minority of pedophile and ephebophile priests have inflicted unspeakable harm and inconsolable heartache on countless children and teenagers, but also because the cult of secrecy and mendacity among the hierarchy, combined with the centuries-old practice of outdated governance and accumulated arrogance, has created an unprecedented crisis of trust in leadership. As a committed Catholic Christian, I have wept with mainline Protestants and evangelical brothers and sisters who are heartbroken over this wound to the Body of Christ. I firmly believe that if we courageously sought a *consensus of the faithful*, the Spirit of God— who speaks through the *whole* Body of Christ—would verify the urgent need of radical Roman reform from the top down, as well as a fearless rethinking of the issues of mandatory celibacy and an all-male priesthood.

Sadly, legalistic religion remains a dimension of the Christian life and spawns a curious species of self-hatred. There are no statistics to help ascertain how many Christians are kept away from the church and deprived of an active spiritual life by the fear-inducing antics of the legalistic mentality, but a college student who wrote to me speaks for them all: "I got involved with a youth group at my church that made me fear for my salvation and be afraid of God. It was a terrorist spirituality, and I decided that there was no point in going to church anymore."

The church, in all its structures and facets, should contribute to the resolution of self-hatred rather than write another chapter for the script. "For it believes in a Father before whom there can be no disgrace. He can have no contempt for us, since our infamies are nothing in his eyes. Yet churchmen have ever been tempted to use people's native shame to maneuver into a position of advantage with them. The Lord whose cherishing should be our greatest source of peace is again and again disfigured by morbid preachers who prefer a god of wrath."[18]

UNHEALTHY GUILT

Healthy guilt adds not a single paragraph to the script for self-hatred. To the contrary, the conviction of personal sinfulness leads to realistic confrontation, ruthless honesty, and self-knowledge; it stimulates compunction, contrition, the desire for reconciliation and inner peace.

As in any lovers' quarrel, the making-up not only absolves the past but brings a new depth of trust and security to the relationship. There is more power in sharing our weaknesses than in sharing our strengths. The forgiveness of God is gratuitous and unconditional, offering liberation from the domination of guilt. God overlooks our past, takes away present or future consequences of past transgressions, and causes us to cry out, "O happy fault!" The sinful and repentant prodigal son experienced an intimacy and joy with his Father in his brokenness that his sinless self-righteous brother would never know.

Perhaps the most powerful charism of the fellowship of Alcoholics Anonymous is to lead its members to full ownership of their brokenness, to publicly acknowledge their failure, to accept responsibility for their humanness. When called upon to speak, the alcoholic begins, "My name is Brennan. I am an alcoholic." There is no hedging, fudging, minimizing, rationalizing, or justifying my sickness. Only a candid admission that once I take that first drink I can neither guarantee my behavior nor predict when I will stop, that I am a victim of an allergy of the body coupled with an obsession of the mind, that I am powerless over alcohol, and that my life has become unmanageable.

The grace of AA is to open my eyes to myself, to give me *healthy* guilt, to tell me things that friends should be telling me but somehow renege because of fear of rejection. AA invites me to confess my weakness at the very moment I am turning away from it. It urges no embarrassment on me. The drunkalogue is a narrative of my ersatz behavior while under the influence and temporary insanity of alcohol. Wittingly or unwittingly, the empathy, compassion, and unconditional acceptance of other drunks give me a glimpse of the unflinching love of the Abba of Jesus, who cannot despise.

These words of German theologian Walter Kasper could have been written with the AA fellowship in mind: "The all-surpassing love of God makes itself felt in the acceptance of human beings by each other, in the dismantling of prejudices and social barriers, in new unrestricted communication among men, in brotherly warmth and the sharing of sadness and joy."[19]

The sharing of healthy guilt is purgative and cathartic, introduces objectivity, banishes self-hatred, and becomes the occasion of gracious encounter with the merciful love of the redeeming God.

When G. K. Chesterton's detective priest, Father Brown, is asked how he could be so astute as to get into a criminal's mind, he answers that it came from the discovery that he is a criminal himself:

> No man's really any good till he knows how bad he is, or might be; till he's realized how much right he has to all this talk of "criminals," as if they were apes in a forest ten thousand miles away; till he's got rid of all the dirty self-deception of talking about low types and deficient skills; till he's squeezed out the last drop of the oil of the Pharisees; till his only hope is somehow or other to have captured one criminal, and kept him safe under his own hat.[20]

Let us suppose that after seven years of marriage a couple has their first serious spat. Tempers flare, hostile words are exchanged, and in a fit of anger the husband slaps his wife, storms out the door, and retreats to the corner saloon. He orders a whiskey and beer chaser and begins to reflect: "I love that woman. She is the warm center of my world. Without her, my life loses meaning, direction, and purpose. And I just blew it. I hurt the one person who means more to me than anyone else. Hell, what am I doing sitting here? Every minute wasted on this barstool could be spent loving her." He leaves his drink untouched, dashes down the street, up the stairs, and with a heart crushed with sorrow falls into his wife's arms.

Healthy guilt is other-centered, arouses compunction and the desire for reconciliation, and calls us into the fullness of humanity by staring in the face defiantly and without embarrassment the gods of pride, arrogance, self-righteousness, and self-pity. "Learn from me," the Master says, "for I am gentle and humble in heart" (Matt. 11:29).

In his riveting book *Shame and Grace*, Lewis Smedes writes,

> Given the crabbed side of my own spirit, my irresistible urge to seek my own interests at the cost of others, my comfort in the teeth of other people's suffering, my niggardly envy of other people's success, and given my urges to smash the nose of any driver who cuts in front of me, given such flaws, am I not more in tune with reality if I accept my shame as the cost of failing to be the self I ought to be, the self I am meant to be, and the self I really want to be? This is healthy shame, and we are closest to health when we let ourselves feel the pain of it and be led by the pain to do something about it.[21]

On the other hand, suppose the husband entrenched on the barstool ruminates, "I claim to be a Christian husband and I just humiliated, insulted, vilified, and physically abused my wife. I'm an elder at my church, and people look up to me as a model Christian. I'm a damn hypocrite!" He orders a double from the bartender. "What have all these years of church-going done for me? Not an ounce of patience, not a whit of understanding. I'm a sewer, I'm a sewer, a great big cesspool." The pity-party and the drinking continue until the desolate husband has neither of his oars in the water, and his drunken little rowboat is finally towed home by other sympathetic sailors in the pub.

Unhealthy guilt is self-centered; it stirs our emotions to churn in self-destructive ways, leads to depression and despair, closes us in upon ourselves, and preempts the presence of a compassionate God. "The language of unhealthy guilt is one of harshness," observes therapist Vincent Bilotta:

> It is demanding, abusive, criticizing, rejecting, finding fault with, accusing, blaming, condemning, reproaching and scolding. It is [a language] of impatience and chastisement. Persons are shocked and horrified because they failed. Unhealthy guilt becomes bigger than life. It is seen as the beginning and the end. In unhealthy guilt, the image of the childhood story "Chicken Little" comes to mind. Guilt becomes the experience in which people feel that the sky is falling.[22]

Smedes makes a careful distinction:

> Spiritual shame may come as a tremor after a close encounter with God, but unhealthy shame is a godless

shame. Undeserved shame may come from religion, but it only gets in God's way. Religion without grace can tie shame around our souls like a choke chain and never offers relief. The pain we feel is not even a distant cousin to spiritual shame.[23]

When God introduces creative tension into our lives by calling us to break camp, abandon the security and comfort of the status quo, and embark in perilous freedom on a new exodus, our insecurity and procrastination may focus only on the darker implications of the challenge and plunge us anew into unhealthy guilt. Stubbornly to stand still when the Lord is clearly challenging us to growth is hard-heartedness, infidelity, and connotes a dangerous lack of trust.

But to start trekking across the desert impulsively without the guidance of the cloud and the fire is reckless folly. When God's call is not clarified and the inner voice remains indistinct, our restlessness and interior disquiet may be signaling a new exodus into greater openness, vulnerability, and compassion, a deeper purity of heart, a transformed mind and spirit. The landscape of the American church is littered with burned-out bodies and abortive ministries born of unhealthy guilt and fear of resisting God's will.

Who will acquit us from guilt? Who will free us from the bondage of projectionism, perfectionism, and moralism? Who will rewrite the script?

Thanks be to God for Jesus Christ our Lord!

NOTES

1. Flannery O'Connor, *The Complete Stories* (New York: Farrar, Strauss & Giroux, 1971), pp. 42–54.
2. O'Connor, *The Complete Stories*, p. 54.
3. Blaise Pascal, *Pensées* (New York: Dutton, 1958), p. 58.
4. James T. Burtchaell, C.S.C., *Philemon's Problem* (Chicago: ACTA Foundation, 1973), p. 18.
5. Burtchaell, *Philemon's Problems*, p. 18.
6. Bernard Bush, "Coping with God" (an inspired essay!), in *Coping: Fifth Boston Psychotheological Symposium* (Whitinsville, MA: Affirmation Books, 1976), p. 28.
7. Bush, "Coping with God," p. 28.
8. Bush, "Coping with God," p. 58.
9. David S. Burns, "The Perfectionist's Script for Self-Defeat, *Psychology Today*, Nov. 1980, p. 34.
10. Gregory Baum, *Religion and Alienation: A Theological Reading of Sociology* (New York: Paulist Press, 1975), p. 68.
11. James Gaffney, *Newness of Life: A Modern Introduction to Catholic Ethics* (New York: Paulist Press, 1979), p. 89.
12. Pascal, *Pensées*, p. 86.
13. Ernst Käsemann, *Jesus Means Freedom* (Philadelphia: Fortress Press, 1969), p. 26.
14. Barbara Doherty, *I Am What I Do: Contemplation and Human Experience* (Chicago: Thomas More Press, 1981), p. 12.
15. John F. O'Grady, *Jesus, Lord and Christ* (New York: Paulist Press, 1973), p. 14.
16. O'Connor, *Complete Stories*, p. 491.
17. Edward Schillebeeckx, *Jesus: An Experiment in Christology* (New York: Seabury Press, 1979), p. 165.
18. Burtchaell, *Philemon's Problem*, p. 18.
19. Walter Kasper, *Jesus the Christ* (New York: Paulist Press, 1977), p. 86.
20. G. K. Chesterton, *The Secret of Father Brown*, quoted in Garry Wills, *St. Augustine* (New York: Lipper/Viking, 1999), p. 136.
21. Lewis Smedes, *Shame and Grace* (San Francisco: HarperSanFrancisco, 1993), p. 75.
22. Vincent Bilotta III, "Guilty: For Betraying Who I Am," *Guilt: Fifth Boston Psychotheological Symposium* (Whitinsville, MA: Affirmation Books, 1980), p. 107.
23. Bilotta III, "Guilty: For Betraying Who I Am," p. 107.

2

JESUS: THE STRANGER
TO SELF-HATRED

Never having attended my high school reunion in the forty-nine years since graduation in February 1952, and motivated by guilt, nostalgia, and curiosity, I returned to Xaverian High School, Brooklyn, New York, in April 2002 for the celebration of our golden jubilee. The reunion was both happy and sad. Seven in our class of forty-four had died.

In the unavoidably intimate setting of a relatively small class, my introvert self, longing to spend the night in a shoe, was summoned to socialize. As the preprandials (Catholic foofarrah for cocktails) multiplied and tongues were lubricated, formalities disappeared, ties got shucked, coats were tossed aside, laughter exploded, and conviviality reigned. The threnody for the Brooklyn Dodgers' departure for Los Angeles, and the treachery of the team's president, Walter O'Malley, wailed into the night. It was a calamity of biblical proportions. Several allusions were made to the "unforgivable sin" against the Holy Spirit. "I'm just glad," my old friend Sal said solemnly, "that Abraham Lincoln wasn't alive to see it."

As the evening progressed, I was asked in Brooklyn patois (the sweetest sound I've ever heard), "What da hell ya been doing wit yerself da last fifty years?" Without a second's hesitation, I answered, "It's been a half-century of sin and grace."

With a twinkle in his eyes, Jack asked, "Would you share a little about da foist part?"

"Yes. I've been a drunk and I've been divorced. I've been sexually promiscuous, faithful during my marriage but unfaithful to celibacy, a liar, envious of the gifts of others, a priest who was insufferably arrogant, a people-pleaser and a braggart (which I'm probably being right now to give you the impression that I'm humble and honest)."

The twinkle vanished. "And part two?"

"By sheer undeserved grace, I've been able to abandon myself in unshaken trust to the compassion and mercy of Jesus Christ."

"I need to talk witchya," Jack whispered. "Can we step outside?"

Who is the Jesus of *your* journey? How would *you* describe the Christ who is the still point of a turning world for so many people and an irrelevancy or embarrassment for countless others?

In the year 451 C.E., the Council of Chalcedon answered that Jesus is the incarnation of the Second Person of the Blessed Trinity. Contemporary theologians offer varied alternatives: Jesus is the man for others, the ethical liberator, the personal Savior, the human face of God. Artists and poets speak of Jesus the clown, the mythological man, and the superstar.

To the question of Jesus, "But who do you say that I am?" (Matt. 16:15) many well-read Christians are competent to articulate the answers that have been given by Mark and Luke, Matthew and John, Augustine and Aquinas, Luther and Calvin, Barth and Bultmann, Moltmann and Rahner. *It is their own answer that we do not hear.* Theologians and biblical scholars cannot answer on our behalf: they cannot supply us with the appropriate images, concepts, and expressions: that would be our personal response to the parable that is the life of Jesus. . . . Each of us is confronted with this "lived parable." How do we understand him? No one else—neither the historical disciplines nor theology nor even the first Christians— can answer that question for us. As we hear the parable, the question is put to us: will we bet our life on it?[1]

The challenge, so keenly put in the New Testament— "Who do you say that I am?"—is addressed to each of us. Who is the Jesus of your own interiority? Describe the Christ that you have personally encountered on the grounds of your own self?

Only a stereotypical answer can be forthcoming if we have not developed a personal relationship with Jesus. We can only repeat pious turns of speech that others have spoken or wave a catechism under children's noses if we have not gained some partial insight, some small glimpse of the inexhaustible richness of the mystery who is Jesus Christ.

Elsewhere I wrote,

The gospel of John is not the gospel of the Kingdom but the gospel of Jesus himself. It is impossible to exaggerate the central position of Jesus in the fourth gospel. Central not merely because he is principal protagonist and teacher, but insofar as he illumines every page of it. . . . The reader is, as it were, blinded by the brilliance of his image and comes away like a man who has looked long at the sun—unable to see anything but its light.[2]

John is concerned with one thing only—the person of Jesus. Do we know him? Everything else fades into twilight and darkness; it becomes irrelevant and is shunted aside. A person's life has meaning only inasmuch as he has prophetic truck with the Nazarene. "There is only Christ: he is everything" (Col. 3:11).

One way that I have come to know Jesus is by empathetic identification with marginal characters in the gospel narrative. My background as a sergeant in the Marine Corps lends to relatively easy rapport with the centurion whose story Matthew relates. Remember the day that Jesus healed the centurion's servant? The military man falls down and says, "Sir, I am not worthy to have you enter under my roof. Just give an order and my boy will get better" (Matt. 8:8). But the most revealing line in that story, according to Matthew, is that "Jesus was astonished." He spun round and cried out, "I tell you solemnly, nowhere in Israel have I found faith like this" (8:10). *At last*, Jesus is saying—*finally* someone who understands me and what I want to be for my people: a Savior of boundless compassion, unbearable forgiveness, infinite patience, and healing love. Will the rest of you let me be who I am and stop imposing your small, silly, and self-styled ideas of who you think I ought to be!

Small wonder that biblical scholar Richard Rohr would say, "The old Baltimore catechism isn't wrong, just inadequate. When it says, 'Man is made to know, love and serve God,' it should read, man is made to know how God longs to love and serve him."[3] Jesus remains Lord by serving us. According to Luke 12:37, the world's Judge on the last day will once more gird himself as a slave: "It will go well with those servants whom the master finds wide-awake on his return. I tell you, he will put on an apron, seat them at table, and proceed to wait on them."

Christian freedom is the joyful acceptance of this unprecedented and scandalous reversal of the world's values. In sovereign liberty to prefer to be the servant rather than the lord of the household, to merrily taunt the gods of power, prestige, honor, and recognition, to refuse to take oneself seriously (or to take seriously anyone who takes *him*self seriously!), to live without gloom by a lackey's agenda, to dance to the tune of a different drummer and be captivated with joy and wonder at the vision and lifestyle of the Ebed Yahweh (Servant of God)—these are the revolutionary attitudes that bear the stamp of genuine and unmistakable discipleship. So central is Jesus' teaching on humble apprenticeship and serving love as the royal road to the Kingdom that at the final judgment, God himself disappears and is visible only in our brothers and sisters: "What you did for those around you, you did for me" (Matt. 25:40).

I would rather be numbered among the little band who have at least learned this from Jesus and the Bible than among the legalizers, moralizers, and hair-splitters who are so busy straining the gnat that they swallow the camel. Would not this radical, revolutionary, and thoroughly orthodox mindset plunge us into a new Pentecost that would renew the face of the earth? There is simply no sense in trumpeting the lordship of Jesus if his attitudes, values, and behavior are not recognizable in our lives.

Mohandas Gandhi said, "I tell the Hindus that their lives will be imperfect if they do not also study reverently the teaching of Jesus." And Jesus taught, "Anyone who wants to be great among you must be your servant, and anyone who wants to be first among you must be your slave, just as the Son of Man came not to be served but to serve, and to give his life as a ransom for many" (Matt. 20:26b–28).

According to the apostle Paul, the only criterion for greatness in the new Israel of God is the faith that expresses itself in love (Gal. 5:6). Paul echoes the teaching of Christ in the Upper Room: "You call me Master and Lord, and rightly; so I am. If I, then, the Lord and Master, have washed your feet, you should wash each other's feet. I have given you an example so that you may copy what I have done for you" (John 13:14–15).

Having the humility and courage to serve is the way to true greatness. When a young Baptist minister finished his doctorate, he told me that he wanted to have an international ministry like mine. At that very moment, unknowingly, he disqualified himself from any role in leadership. Ambition to be a star in the Body of Christ is alluring and seductive; it is also demonic, the glamorous enemy of servanthood and love. The steady erosion of servant leadership in the North American church, the deference shown to charismatic superstars, and the bowing and scraping to TV evangelists deface the image of the servant Jesus and make the credibility of Christian leadership literally incredible.

Love is service. "There is no point in getting into an argument about this question of loving. It is what Christianity is all about—take it or leave it. Christianity is not about ritual and moral living except insofar as these two express the love that causes both of them. We must at least pray for the grace to become love."[4]

The spell of self-hatred cast by moralism/legalism is broken when a Christian is no longer seduced by secular standards of human greatness and makes the glorious breakthrough into the lackey lifestyle of the Master, desiring to serve rather than be served. The stark realism of the gospel allows for no romanticized idealism or sloppy sentimentality here. Servanthood is not an emotion or mood or feeling; it's a decision to live the life of Jesus. It has nothing to do with what we *feel;* it has everything to do with what we *do*—humble service. When this metanoia is achieved in our lives by the power of the Spirit, freedom from the tyranny of self-hatred is the first fruit. "It was for liberty that Christ freed us. So stand firm and do not take on yourselves the yoke of slavery a second time" (Gal. 5:1).

"There is no church on earth, no evangelist, no accident of time or culture that could create a man or a message like this.

To listen carefully to these words is to draw close to the Jesus of the Gospels."[5]

During an extended silent retreat in Tampa, Florida, some years ago, I was reading the Scriptures in my room at the Franciscan Retreat Center. The subtle dominion of self-hatred had returned, and I was back on the rollercoaster ride of perfectionist depression, neurotic guilt, and emotional instability. The despotic power of my idealized self and the nagging litany of "I should have, I could have, I ought to have, Why didn't I? Why did I?" had persuaded me that my life and ministry were vitiated by vanity, insensitivity, and self-centeredness.

At that very moment Jesus set me free.

Praying over the passage of the washing of the feet (John 13:1–17), I was suddenly transported in faith into the Upper Room, where I took Judas's place among the Twelve. The Servant, who had tied a towel round his waist, poured water from a pitcher into a copper basin and reached out to wash my feet (the dress and duty those of a slave). Involuntarily I pulled my foot back. I couldn't look at him. I had betrayed the vision, been unfaithful to my dream (and thus unfaithful to his plan for my life).

Sensing my dismay, he placed his hand on my knee and said, "Brennan, do you know what these years together have meant to me? You were being held even when you didn't believe I was holding you. I love you, my friend."

Tears rolled down my cheeks. "But Lord, my sins, my repeated failures, my weaknesses . . . "

"I understand. Brennan, I expected more failure from you

than you expected from yourself." He smiled. "And you always came back. Nothing pleases me as much as when you trust me, when you allow that my compassion is bigger than your sinfulness."

"But Jesus, what about my irritating character defects—the boasting, the inflating of the truth, the pretense of being an intellectual, the impatience with people, and all the times I drank to excess?"

"What you are saying is true. But your love for me has never wavered: your heart has remained pure. What's more, even in the darkness and confusion, you've always done something that overshadowed all the rest. You were kind to sinners."

I cried—so loudly that the retreatant in the adjacent room knocked on the door to ask if I was all right.

"Now I'll go," Jesus said. "I've just washed your feet. Do the same for others. Serve my people humbly and lovingly. You will find happiness if you do. Peace, my friend."

Jesus, a man like us in all things but ungratefulness, our brother who never knew sin, estranges us from self-hatred through a love that keeps no score of wrongs and a mercy that surpasses human understanding. In the eyes of the Master whom we have failed, we detect the infinite compassion of the Father and see revealed, in Jesus, the human face of God.

John O'Grady writes,

The savior knows that we have failures, even when we have committed ourselves to him. The savior redeems us from all personal failure by telling his followers that in spite of our sin we have value in the eyes of God the Father. A new possibility exists. We can be more than we are at any one moment; we can always bring some sense of goodness to the fore and come closer to living the way that will bring us peace. Even in the midst of personal failure the one who has been saved knows that he or she is still precious in the eyes of God, of Jesus and of his holy community. The one who has been saved knows no sense of isolation. Jesus is the friend who will never fail, the faithful one who will never be lacking in fidelity, even when people are unfaithful to him.[6]

The gospel portrait of Jesus is that of a strikingly cheerful person who cherishes life and existence, and especially other people, as loving gifts from the Father's hand. The peripheral figures that Jesus encounters in his ministry react in various ways to his presence and message but never with gloom or sadness. In a remarkable passage, Edward Schillebeeckx explains the non-fasting of the disciples:

Fasting was a sign of mourning and sorrow. It was not that his disciples *did not* fast; they *could not* fast. This was not a matter of liberal dispensation. It was a question of the existential impossibility of being sad in the living presence of Jesus! The sinners and lowlife rejects found that sharing a meal with the Master was a liberating experience of sheer joy. He estranged them from self-hatred with reassuring words such as, "Do not live in fear, little flock; don't be afraid. Fear is useless—stop worrying; cheer up—your sins are all forgiven." His contagious joy (only carriers can pass on) in the lavish, gratuitous, and indiscriminate love of his heavenly Father infected and liberated his listeners. (If Jesus sat at your dining-room table tonight with full knowledge of everything you are and are not; if he laid out your whole lifestory, with the hidden agenda and the dark desires unknown even to yourself, it would still be impossible to be saddened in his presence.)[7]

"Experiencing God's love in Jesus Christ means experiencing that one has been unreservedly accepted, approved and infinitely loved, that one can and should accept oneself and one's neighbor," writes theologian Walter Kasper. "Salvation is joy in God which expresses itself in joy in and with one's neighbor."[8]

To me it is unthinkable to picture a wooden-faced, stoic, and joyless Jesus as he blesses the little children. To perceive the human personality of Jesus as a purely passive mask for the dramatic speeches of divinity is to rob him of his humanity, encase him in plaster of Paris, and conclude that he neither laughed, cried, smiled, nor got hurt, but simply passed through our world without emotional engagement.

The evangelist Mark records that a group of parents, who obviously sensed something of God's love in Jesus, wanted him to bless their little ones. The irritated disciples, fatigued by the long day's journey on foot from Capernaum to the district of Judea on the far side of the Jordan, attempted to shoo away the children. Jesus became visibly upset and perhaps with a withering glance silenced the Twelve. Mark carefully notes that Jesus picked the children up one by one, cradled them, and gave each of them his blessing.

Evangelist Robert Frost comments,

> I am so glad Jesus didn't suggest they group all the children together for a sort of general blessing because he was rather tired. Instead, he took time to hold each child close to his heart and to earnestly pray for them all . . . then they joyfully scampered off to bed. One is tenderly reminded of a beautiful messianic passage from the prophets: "He will feed his flock like a shepherd, he will gather his lambs in his arm, he will carry them in his bosom, and will gently lead those that have their young" (Isa. 40:11, TAB). . . . I think there is a lesson here for anyone who would seek to set any kind of false condition concerning just who should be the recipients of God's grace. He blessed them all![9]

It is staggering, it is mind-blowing, but it is true. Jesus takes the initiative in seeking out the ungodly, even on Sunday morning. His loving visitation ends ungodliness and makes the sinner worthy. It is difficult to understand how anyone has the right to declare limited access to the eucharistic table so that certain people cannot come to Jesus without their consent and approval. Surely there would be abuses, but abuses do not take away the reality. "In Jesus the goodness outweighed the evil that surrounded him. Sinners are always welcome; tax collectors, prostitutes and anyone else who feels left out can find company with Jesus as the forgiving savior. . . . [N]o one was excluded; no one need feel left out."[10]

What would the church be like if we erred from an excess of compassion rather than from a stingy and legalistic lack of it? My intuition is that the Christian community would share something of the mystical vision of Juliana of Norwich, who uttered what may be the loveliest and most consoling sentence I've ever read: "And all thing shall be well; and all thing shall be well; and all manner of thing shall be well!"[11]

Jesus perceived that the only way to help people experience life as gracious gift, the only way to help them to prize themselves as grace and treasure, was to treat them as treasure and be gracious to them. I can be anointed, prayed over, sermonized to, dialogued with, and exposed to God's unconditional love in books, tracts, and tapes, but this marvelous revelation will fall on ears that do not hear and eyes that do not see, unless some other human being refresh the weariness of my defeated days. Barring prevenient grace, we humans simply will not accept our life and being as God's gracious gift unless someone values us. "We can only sense ourselves and our world valued and cherished by God when we feel valued and cherished by others."[12]

One of the most beautiful chapters in the script that is the story of Jesus of Nazareth addresses his relationship with the unnamed sinful woman in Luke's gospel. (A brief digression: one night in Clearwater, Florida, I decided to go to an AA meeting at Indian Rocks Beach. Driving along a two-lane highway that bordered the Gulf of Mexico, I picked up a twenty-year-old female hitchhiker. After a perfunctory greeting, she proceeded to tell me of her resentment for her live-in boyfriend. Both were heavy cocaine users, she said, and he demanded that she prostitute herself with his friends to support their habit. I asked her, "Have you turned to God and asked him to help you?" In a breezy, nonchalant voice she replied, "Oh, I know that God loves me." But she did *not* know. All she had was a memory from childhood—vague, abstract, and as unreal as little George Washington chopping down the cherry tree. But she *could* experience God in a real way and come to see her life as gracious gift if her unchained boyfriend would treasure her the way Jesus treasured the sinful woman in the home of Simon the Pharisee (Luke 7:36–50).)

This is the Christ of my own interiority, the Deliverer from self-hatred through love. At a dinner in the home of Simon the Pharisee, the unnamed sinful woman was awed by the loveliness and compassion that streamed from Jesus' face. His eyes called out to her, "Come to me. Come now. Don't wait until you have your act cleaned up and your head on straight. Don't delay until you think you are properly disposed and free of pride and lust, jealousy and self-hatred. Come to me in your brokenness and sinfulness, with all your fears and insecurities, and I will comfort you. I will come to you *right where you live* and love you just the way you are, and not the way you think you *should* be."

Jesus convinced her that "winter had passed, that the rains were over and gone" (Song of Sol. 2:11), that her sins had been forgiven and that God now accepted her and approved of her. The moment she surrendered in faith, love took effect and her life was transformed. The result was the inner healing of her heart manifested as peace, joy, gratitude, and love. The love of Christ called the sinful woman to enter into the mystery of herself, to abandon clarity—"the kind of clarity the ego seeks, the kind of clarity which comforts me and allows me to think that all I really am is what I *think* I am, and that's all there is to it."[13]

The creative power of Jesus' love called the repentant woman to regard herself as he did, to see in herself the possibilities that he saw in her.

> The place that this transformed woman occupies in Christian thought is not due to her strange, deep love for Jesus, but rather to what was wrought in her by Christ's love for her. It was Christ's love for her that delivered her from her past and made her what she became. The central truth for which her life has come to stand is that it is possible to be delivered, through love, from the lowest depths to the shining heights where God dwelleth.[14]

The same theme is replayed with Peter. The compassion of Jesus reaches its zenith in their dialogue on the shores of the Sea of Tiberias. Only the risen Lord could sound the depths of Peter's hurt, guilt, and self-hatred. Only Jesus fully understood that there was no treachery in Peter's denial—just a temporary loss of nerve. Like a Marine in combat for the first time, the instinct for self-preservation had prevailed. Yet in spite of that betrayal, the purity of Peter's heart and the quality of his love were not debatable or open to question in spite of his betrayal. Jesus had to rid the apostle of his clarity, of his limited self-perception, of the debased self-image of who he thought he was.

There would be healing from self-hatred for Peter that morning.

Jesus said, "Simon, son of John, do you love me more than these?" "Yes, Lord," he said, "you know that I love you." At which Jesus said, "Feed my lambs." A second time he put his question, "Simon, son of John, do you love me?" "Yes, Lord," Peter said, "you know that I love you." Jesus replied, "Tend my sheep." A third time Jesus asked him, "Simon, son of John, do you love me?"

Peter was hurt because he had asked a third time, "Do you love me?" So he said to him, "Lord, you know everything. You know well that I love you."

Jesus said to him, "Feed my sheep" (John 21:15–17).

Jesus not only frees Peter from self-hatred by allowing him to publicly repudiate his triple denial, but in the subtlest act of affirmation conceivable he appoints him leader of his church and entrusts him to preach the Good News with supreme authority in the power of the Spirit.

"I don't know what Peter felt at that moment, but if it's anything like I have experienced with the Lord, it is like this," biblical scholar George Montague writes,

> God, I don't even know how to be a fisher of men, now you want me to be a shepherd. I don't even know how to fish, Lord, without you, how am I going to shepherd

these people? I don't know how. Jesus didn't say anything more; what he said was enough. Do you love me?
Can you allow my love to touch you in your weakness,
and set you free there, and empower you? So that when
Peter went out from then on empowered by Jesus, *the
only power he had was Jesus' love for him* and his love for the
Lord. That's the only power that he had. Jesus wanted to
strip him even of his power to fish, and of any of his
other self-confidences except that God is love and God's
power has been given to me in my weakness. Peter told
and retold the story of his own weakness and how the
Lord touched him. When Peter preached, he preached
from his weakness the power of God. And that is what
converted the Roman world and what will convert us,
and the people around us if they see that the power of
God has touched us.[15]

The unflinching, unwavering love and compassion of Jesus
Christ, the stranger to self-hatred, is the ultimate source of
our healing and wholeness. This was the experience of Jesus'
followers. This was the kind of impact he had upon them.
This is the real Jesus inscribed on every page of the gospels. If
we wish to treat Jesus as our God, we must let him be who he
wants to be for us. Returning to Rohr's observation, we have
to conclude that we are made to know how God longs to love
and serve us, to free and forgive, to heal and make whole his
children.

Does the church have any more urgent ministry than pro-
viding time and making space for the critical question of the

Christ in John's gospel: "Do you love me?" Is there any creedal, codal, or cultic priority that supersedes the personal relationship between the believer and Jesus Christ? Is there any hope for radical Christian renewal and the implementation of the social gospel if Jesus Christ is not Lord of my life? Do we set this decisive question aside in favor of moralizing, philosophizing, organizing, and erecting new temples to an unknown god?

"The criterion by which Christ assesses his friends and repudiators is still 'Do you love me?' What do we make of the Bible if we forget this, even if we hold to everything else? How can one muster the melancholy courage, the incredible hard-heartedness, and the insipid stupidity, to inflate demythologizing, historical criticism, and existentialist interpretation into such a bogey that Jesus' question takes a back place?"[16]

My own glimpse of Jesus moved from obscurity to increasing clarity on a winter's night, December 13, 1968, in the Zaragoza desert in Spain. I was living in a cave six thousand feet above the village of Farlete, it was 3:00 A.M., and the world was asleep, but my heart was awake to God. During what began as a long and lonely hour of prayer, I heard Jesus say, "For love of you I left my Father's side. I came to you who ran from me, who fled me, who did not want to hear my name. For love of you I was covered with spit, punched and beaten, and fixed to the wood of the cross."

Although it was thirty-five years ago, this morning in an hour of quiet time, I realized that those words still burned on my life. Whether I am in a state of grace or disgrace, the words impose themselves with the stark realism of objective truth. That night in the cave I stared at a crucifix for hours, figuratively seeing the blood streaming from every wound and pore in Christ's body; and I heard the cry of his blood: "This is not a joke. It is not a laughing matter to me that I have loved you." The longer I looked, the more I realized that no man has ever loved me and no woman could ever love me as he does. I cried out in the darkness, "Jesus, are you crazy—are you out of your mind to have loved me so much?" I learned that night what a wise old Franciscan told me the day I joined the Order: "Once you come to know the love of Jesus Christ, nothing else in the world will seem beautiful or desirable."

Ironically, it was the same day, December 13, twelve years later that I went to pray in the parish church in Tamarac, Florida, at two in the afternoon. The usual tenor of my prayer-life is dryness, longing, and experiencing the absence of God in the hope of communion. But the moment I knelt down my mind was filled with the image of a three-year-old boy playing on the rug in his living room. Off in the corner his mother sat on the floor in the lotus position, knitting. Suddenly she dropped her work and beckoned to him. He toddled over and climbed up on her lap. She smiled down at him and asked softly, "How much do you love me?" He extended his tiny arms as far as they would go and exclaimed, "*This much* I love you." In an instant, it was thirty-some years later; the little boy in the fullness of manhood hung nailed to a crossbeam. His mother looked up and said, "How much do you love me?" His arms were stretched out to the ends of the universe. "*This much* I love you." And he died.

We turn once again to the pivotal question: Who is Jesus? Everything else is a distraction. He is the crucified one. "He is unmistakable and identifiable with Jesus of Nazareth only as the man of the cross." It is the signature of the risen one, and it follows that a Christian is only a disciple as long as he stands in the shadow of the cross.

It is inevitable that when you hang with bad company, you get a bad reputation. Is there anything more precious to us than our good name? Our standing in the community is not a minor matter to any of us. What would people think if you were frequently seen in the company of prostitutes, drug dealers, and slumlords?

Jesus mixed easily with the nobodies, the discards, and the lowlife rejects. He mingled with tax collectors who were downright sinners—"miserable sinners in the proper sense of the term, practicing a proscribed trade, odious cheats and swindlers, grown rich in the service of the occupying power, afflicted with permanent uncleanness as collaborators and traitors to the national cause, incapable of repentance because they simply could not remember how many they had cheated or how much was involved. And such professional swindlers were the very people with whom Jesus had to get involved."[17]

Biblical scholar Albert Nolan comments on Jesus' outrageous consorting with sinners:

He was not afraid of creating a scandal or losing his reputation or even losing his life. All the men of religion, even John the Baptist, were scandalized by the way he mixed socially with sinners, by the way he seemed to

enjoy their company, by his permissiveness with regard
to the laws, by his apparent disregard for the seriousness
of sin and by his free and easy way of treating God. . . .
Jesus did nothing and compromised on nothing for the
sake of even a modicum of prestige in the eyes of others.
He did not seek anyone's approval, not even the
approval of the greatest man born of woman.[18]

Two millennia later I find myself threatened, challenged,
and exhilarated by Christ's freedom from human respect, by
his extraordinary independence, indomitable courage, and unparalleled authenticity. In preaching the gospel I have been
graced to speak fearlessly in the knowledge and conviction
that the Word of God must not be fettered, compromised, or
watered down; but in my personal life, my fears and insecurities continue to lead me voraciously to seek the approval of
others, to assume a defensive posture when I'm unjustly
accused, to feel guilty over refusing any request, to doggedly
live up to others' expectations, to be all things to all people in
a way that would make St. Paul shudder.

Powerful others will try to make me conform and live up
to their expectations. I may have to run the risk of being
defiant, of standing up to, and of going against powerful
others. I am called to stand on my own two feet and to
develop the ability to say yes or no in making decisions
for the emergence of my life. To be seduced from following my path is to be controlled by others, to become
a people pleaser, and to be ruled by the tyrannical

demands of others. Failure to stand up to others and to assume responsibility for the direction of my life and the promotion of love in light of God's design for me should engender healthy guilt.[19]

I cannot free myself. I must be set free. Yes, the untrammeled freedom of Jesus disturbs me, his utter indifference to human respect makes me uncomfortable; but he invites me to make friends with my insecurities, smile at them, outgrow them in patient endurance, live with the serene confidence that he never abandons his friends even when we disappoint him, and look forward in expectant faith to the day when I can say to the angry chairperson of the Inscrutable Noonies Society, whose speaking invitation I have just refused, "Frankly, my dear, I don't give a damn!"

It can be unequivocally stated that the central, most important theme in the personal life of Jesus—the theme that lies at the very heart of the revelation that he is—is his growing trust, intimacy, and love of his Abba, his heavenly Father. The interior life of Christ was completely Father-centered. The master clue for interpreting the gospel narrative, the foundation of Jesus' compelling demands, the source of his towering zeal—was his personal experience of God as Abba. "The overtones of this small word will always remain beyond us, yet we sense in it something of the closeness of Jesus with his Father. We touch in it the very heart of his personality. The Abba experience made him the person he was. It freed him from all self-concern and enabled him to relate to each and every person with great ease, openness, sympathy and a liberating love."[20]

The pearl of great price in my life, the most treasured gift I've ever received from Jesus is to come to know the Father. "No one knows the Son except the Father, just as no one knows the Father except the Son and those to whom the Son chooses to reveal him" (Matt. 11:27). Biblical scholar Joachim Jeremias did not hesitate to call this the central revelation of the New Testament.

Jesus brought a revolution in the understanding of God. It is impossible to exaggerate the extravagance of the Father's compassion and love. The god of Ruller—Something Awful—and all other false images are blown away. Projection is exposed for the idolatry that it is. To pray to any god other than a Father who finds sheer delight in reconciliation is illusion, cowardice, and superstition. For the disciple, God is no other than as he is seen in the person of Jesus: "He who sees me sees the Father" (John 14:9).

The love of the Father for his children plunges us into mystery, because it is utterly beyond the pale of human experience. The parable of the prodigal son reveals a love that is gratuitous. Let us suppose that you financed your youngest son through an Ivy League university—room, board, tuition, spending money, and plane tickets home to the tune of sixty thousand dollars over four years. He graduates. You host a lavish party for two hundred of his friends and classmates—champagne and caviar, pizza and Ripple wine, baked Alaska and Twinkies. Britney Spears, 'N Sync, and U2 are flown in to provide the music. The celebration breaks up at dawn. You sit before the fireplace with your son and inquire whether he enjoyed the night.

"I'm going to level with you," he answers. "I can't stand you, your values, or your face. Tomorrow my insurance policy matures and I'm splitting. I've got my diploma, and that's my passport to fat city."

You are stunned and brokenhearted, but you know you cannot stop him. For the next three years, you literally do not know if he is dead or alive. No calls or postcards: the police cannot find a trace of him.

Then one Monday morning at 3:00 A.M. your doorbell rings. Groggy, you trip downstairs and open the door in shock. Your son is standing on the steps, booze on his breath, lipstick on his collar, his clothes disheveled.

If you were that father, what would you do at your prodigal's return? Would you fall on your son's neck, smother him with tears and kisses, throw on the lights, and summon your spouse from upstairs by shouting, "Break out the Dom Perignon we've been saving and put on Handel's *Messiah*. Bobby's home! He's not dead; he's alive!"

Your neighbors would undoubtedly inform you that your cheese had just slid off your cracker! But Jesus says, "That is the way my Father is. He wants you home more than you want to be home. His love knows no bounds. Never compare your pallid, capricious, conditional human love with my Father's love. He is God, not man."

Try, if you please, to invent a different ending for this story. Make the old man rebuff the boy at first; have him stand on his dignity and require of the rascal proofs of his change of heart; let him read a sermon on wild oats before the forgiving kiss is bestowed; have him take the penitent at his word—as he richly deserves to be taken—and try him out with the slaves for a year or two, till the family pride, or outraged justice, is satisfied. Imagine, in short, *any possible ending but this*, and you have destroyed the noblest picture of redeeming grace ever created, and lowered God to the level of man's virtue. Heathen religions in plenty, and some versions of the Christian religion, furnish us with the alternatives suggested above; Christ alone shows us the suffering Father who saves by forgiving.[21]

Jesus is the human face of that suffering, loving, forgiving Father.

Though it is remarkably easy to call God "Abba," it is almost impossible to live faithfully and steadfastly as his beloved child. To pray, "thy will be done" from the bowels of your being requires a great deal. (It cost Jesus his life.) To do the perceived will of God in all circumstances and relationships enjoins radical obedience to the Word who said, "I come to do your will, O God." It was Jesus' food and he demands the same diet of his followers.

The phrase "Thy will be done" occurs in only four places in the New Testament—all in the context of martyrdom.[22] The three passion narratives in the synoptic gospels refer explicitly to Jesus' impending death. Paul announces that he is ready for martyrdom in Acts 21:13–14: "'Why are you crying and breaking my heart in this way? For the name of the Lord Jesus I am prepared not only for imprisonment, but for death, in

Jerusalem.' Since [Paul] would not be dissuaded, [the disciples] said nothing further except, 'The Lord's will be done.'" For Paul, death was not terminal; rather, it would be the final breakthrough into the open, waiting, outstretched arms of the Abba of Jesus. In the noncanonical writing known as *The Martyrdom of Polycarp*, the soldiers seize Polycarp and begin to beat him about the face and body. He cries out, "May God's will be done," and the martyrdom begins.

The Father's will is a river of life flowing into Jesus, inundating his being. It is a bloodstream from which he draws life even more profoundly than he draws life from his mother. And whoever stands at the ready in obedient love becomes a part of this bloodstream. The disciple is united to Jesus more deeply even than the way in which Jesus was united to his mother.

To acknowledge that our Father is the source of all life and holiness makes gratitude the most characteristic attitude of the child of God. The petition "Give us this day our daily bread" expresses our creaturely dependence and the acceptance of all of life as God's gracious gift. It strikes down possessiveness and makes us conscious that we are beggars.

And yet how reluctant we are to receive the gift! We stake out our piece of turf, claim it as our own, become grasping, anxious, and care-ridden about the security of our baubles, trinkets, golf balls, and immaculate lawns. "We gather into barns, insure the barns and their contents, buy a German shepherd or hire a security guard, and try to see to it that Blacks do not build barns in the same area."[23] We sell ourselves to the gods of security, sensation, and power, and a sickness enters the very heart of our existence. We grow competitive rather than compassionate, make others our rivals, stepping-stones to our enthronement in a palace overlooking Malibu, part of life's expense account, enslaved in the Babylonian captivity of the modern world.

One does not find an attitude of gratitude in the slave market.

Jesus brings freedom from the money game, the power game, the pleasure game, and the pervasive sense of self-hatred that racks our torn conscience. With insight that defies imagination, he proposes a new agenda that proffers peace and a joy that the world would never dare promise: "Turn to my Father, set your heart on his kingdom, and these other things will be given you as well" (Luke 12:31).

This is a glimpse of the Jesus whom I have met over the years on the terrain of my wounded self, the Christ of my interiority. There is a beauty and enchantment about the Nazarene that draws me irresistibly to follow him. He is the Pied Piper of my lonely heart. It is not pious prattle to say that the only valid reason I can think of for living is Jesus Christ. Paul puts it so well: "There is only Christ, and he is everything" (Col. 3:11).

In order to be free to be faithful to this sacred man and his dream, to others and ourselves, we must be liberated from the damnable imprisonment of self-hatred, freed from the shackles of projectionism, perfectionism, moralism/legalism, and unhealthy guilt. Freedom for fidelity demands freedom from enslavement.

It's a tired cliché, a battered bumper sticker, an overused and often superficial slogan, but it's the truth of the gospel:

A GLIMPSE OF JESUS

Jesus is the answer. Is there any price too exorbitant, any cost too extravagant to pay for the privilege of being able to make your own personal response to his haunting question: Who do you say that I am? "I believe that nothing can happen that will outweigh the supreme advantage of knowing Christ Jesus my Lord . . . and I look on everything else as rubbish if only I can have Christ" (Phil. 3:8).

NOTES

1. Edward Schillebeeckx, *Jesus: An Experiment in Christology* (New York: Seabury Press, 1979), pp. 171–172, italics added.
2. Ernst Käsemann, *Jesus Means Freedom* (Philadelphia: Fortress Press, 1969), p. 155.
3. Source unknown.
4. Barbara Doherty, *I Am What I Do: Contemplation and Human Experience* (Chicago: Thomas More Press, 1981), p. 211.
5. Donald Senior, C.P., *Jesus: A Gospel Portrait* (Cincinnati: Pflaum Standard, 1975), p. 57.
6. John F. O'Grady, *Models of Jesus* (Garden City, NY: Doubleday, 1981), pp. 146–147.
7. Schillebeeckx, *Jesus*, pp. 204–205.
8. Walter Kasper, *Jesus the Christ* (New York: Paulist Press, 1977), p. 86.
9. Robert Frost, *Our Heavenly Father* (Plainfield, NJ: Logos, 1978), p. 44.
10. O'Grady, *Models of Jesus*, p. 161.
11. Quoted in Anthony de Mello, S.J., *Sadhana: A Way to God* (St. Louis: Institute of Jesuit Sources, 1978), p. 134.
12. James P. Mackey, *Jesus: The Man and the Myth* (New York: Paulist Press, 1979), p. 170.
13. Tad Guzie and John McIlhon, *The Forgiveness of Sin* (Chicago: Thomas More Press, 1979), p. 38.
14. Cynthia Pearl Maus, *Christ and the Fine Arts* (New York: Harper & Row, 1938), p. 215.
15. George Montague, C.M., italics added. This quote is taken from his teaching on healing at the charismatic conference, Notre Dame, IN, May 1981.
16. Käsemann, *Jesus Means Freedom*, p. 147.
17. Hans Küng, *On Being a Christian* (New York: Doubleday, 1976), p. 271.
18. Albert Nolan, O.P., *Jesus Before Christianity* (Maryknoll, NY: Orbis Books, 1976), pp. 117–118.

19.   Vincent Bilotta III, "Guilty: For Betraying Who I Am," *Guilt: Fifth Boston Psycho-theological Symposium* (Whitinsville, MA: Affirmation Books, 1980), p. 109.

20.   Peter van Breemen, S.J., *Certain as the Dawn*. The author is quoting from his previous work, *Called by Name* (Denville, NJ: Dimension Books, 1980), p. 31.

21.   Albert E. Bailey, author of *The Gospel in Art*, quoted in Maus, *Christ and the Fine Arts*, p. 173.

22.   This discussion is based on notes taken at a series of lectures titled *The Prayer of Jesus*, given by Father Francis Martin at Loyola University, New Orleans, July 1978.

23.   Mackey, *Jesus*, pp. 135–136.

3

HEALING THROUGH
MEAL-SHARING

In the year 1925, if a wealthy plantation owner in Atlanta, Georgia, had extended a formal invitation to four colored cotton-pickers to come to his mansion for Sunday dinner, preceded by cocktails and followed by several hours of brandy and conversation, the Georgia aristocracy would have been outraged, neighboring Alabama infuriated, and the KKK apoplectic. The caste system was inviolable, social and racial discrimination inflexible, and indiscretion made the loss of reputation inevitable.

The scandal that Jesus caused in first-century Palestinian Judaism can scarcely be appreciated by the Christian world today. The class system was enforced *de rigueur*. It was legally forbidden to mingle with sinners who were outside the law; the prohibition on table-fellowship with beggars, prostitutes, and tax-collectors was a religious, social, and cultural taboo.

Theologian Marcus Borg notes that "one of the most striking features of Jesus' ministry [was] the meals he shared with 'sinners'—that is, outcasts. Pharisees (and others) would not eat with somebody who was impure, and no decent person would share a meal with an outcast."[1] When Jesus ate with tax-collectors as well, the religious satraps were infuriated, because "tax collectors were among the worst of the untouchables."[2]

Unfortunately, the meaning of meal-sharing is largely lost on Western society today. In the East, to share a meal with someone is a symbol of peace, trust, brotherhood, and forgiveness; the shared table is a shared life. To say to an Orthodox Jew, "I would like to have dinner with you," is understood as "I would like to enter into friendship with you."

Even today, members of Orthodox Jewry will share a donut and a cup of coffee with you, but when they extend a dinner invitation, they are saying, "Come to my *mikdash me-at*, my miniature sanctuary, my dining-room table, and we will celebrate the most beautiful experience that life affords—friendship." That is what Zacchaeus heard when Jesus called him down from the sycamore tree, and that is why Jesus' practice of table-fellowship caused hostile comment from the outset of his ministry.

It did not escape the Pharisees' attention that Jesus meant to befriend the rabble. He was not only breaking the law; he was destroying the very structure of Jewish society! "They all complained when they saw what was happening. He has gone to stay at a sinner's house, they said" (Luke 19:7). But Zacchaeus, not too hung up on respectability, was overwhelmed with joy.

It would be impossible to overestimate the impact these meals must have had upon the poor and the sinners. By accepting them as friends and equals Jesus had taken away their shame, humiliation and guilt. By showing them that they mattered to him as people he gave them a sense of dignity and released them from their old captivity. The physical contact which he must have had with them at table (John 13:25) and which he obviously never dreamed of disallowing (Luke 7:38–39) must have made them feel clean and acceptable. Moreover because Jesus was looked upon as a man of God and a prophet, they would have interpreted his gesture of friendship as God's approval of them. They were now acceptable to God. Their sinfulness, ignorance and uncleanness had been overlooked and were no longer being held against them.[3]

Through table-fellowship Jesus ritually acted out his insight into the Father's indiscriminate love—a love that causes his sun to rise on bad people as well as good, and his rain to fall on the honest and the dishonest alike (Matt. 5:45). The inclusion of sinners in the community of salvation, achieved in table-fellowship, is the most dramatic expression of the message of the redeeming love of the merciful God.

Several years ago German theologian Karl Rahner was giving a lecture in Rome on salvation and remarked that salvation "is a bottle of coke." All over Europe there are signs: things go better with coke. Rahner described the experience,

The day is hot and the streets of Rome are dusty and filled with exhaust from the buses; you walk along with your friend, you see the sign, sit down and enjoy the

comfort and ease of a bottle of coke with your friend.
Salvation is a bottle of coke.[4]

O'Grady writes,

Whatever contributes to the well-being of mankind, whatever is good and noble and lovely and true is the experience of salvation. Salvation is not reserved for the future
alone. It is present when a family sits down at a family celebration in thanksgiving for the goodness they have
received and the goodness they contribute to each other
and enjoy fine food and good wine and great company.[5]

The ordinary meal-sharing of Jesus at home and on the
road was Eucharist, and so should be the thousand meals that
a family shares each year. The early eucharistic meals were
grateful celebrations of God's gift of life, celebrated in shared
food and joyful fellowship. It seems to have been Jesus'
favorite form of recreation. Dinner parties were such a prominent aspect of his routine that, more than once, he was
accused of being a drunkard and a glutton (e.g., Luke 7:34).
   The thorough research of biblical scholar Albert Nolan
indicates that Jesus had his own home in Capernaum, or at
least a *communal* home, shared with Peter, Andrew, and their
families. Undoubtedly, in his ministry of itinerant evangelism,
Jesus often slept on the side of the road or stayed with friends.
"The Son of man has nowhere to lay his head" (Mark 8:20).
But upon returning from his missionary journeys, he had some
kind of quasi-permanent domicile.[6] The phrase "he *entertained*

sinners" (Luke 15:2) suggests that Jesus was often the host and may have rented a hall more than once (as he did at the Last Supper). The guest list would include a ragtag parade of donkey peddlers, prostitutes, herdsmen, slumlords, and gamblers. A social climber Jesus was not!

Status-seekers in today's society are selective about their dinner guests and make elaborate preparations for people they want to stand well with. They wait anxiously to see if they will be invited in return. Consciously or unconsciously, the power brokers and social gadflys of our day do not underestimate the ritual power of meal-sharing. Jesus' sinner-guests were well aware that table-fellowship entailed more than mere politeness and courtesy; it meant peace, acceptance, reconciliation, fraternity. As Hans Küng notes, "For Jesus this fellowship at table with those whom the devout had written off was not merely the expression of liberal tolerance and humanitarian sentiment. It was the expression of his mission and message: peace and reconciliation for all, without exception, even for the moral failures."[7]

I once met a pastor in the hills of Colorado who invites a family to his rectory every Sunday afternoon for a homecooked meal. Frequently the guests are unchurched or exchurched. During my visit the fare was simple, but the company and conversation stimulating. This family shared the deep hurt inflicted on them by a previous pastor and why they consequently had discontinued churchgoing. But that afternoon they received consideration instead of expected condemnation, a merciful acquittal rather than an anticipated verdict of guilty. They returned to the worshiping community the following week.

They had been healed by an ordinary Sunday meal! Table-sharing with the pastor had brought them into fellowship with God.

How do we justify the exclusion of divorced Christians from the Lord's Supper, when Jesus hosted sinners and set the table for moral failures? How long is this really to go on? Within the Roman Catholic discipline, the conditions and requirements for obtaining an annulment have been widened and broadened. "Although this procedure has been a source of some relief, it is clearly a legal makeshift, open to serious abuses, and basic problems in this area remain difficult and urgent."[8]

A sixty-eight-year-old man from Florida came to me for counseling; in fact, he fell into my arms in tears. He had been deprived of table-fellowship and the taking of communion for forty-six years! Even the incestuous man in Corinth was permitted to return to the faith community lest he fall into despair. Wounded at Anzio Beach in World War II, he had been honorably discharged and had returned to the States. In desperate loneliness he had married a girl he barely knew in a Christian ceremony. Within three weeks she had committed adultery with several other men, and thus the marriage had ended in divorce. This man had remarried outside the church, and, as so often happens, the second, successful marriage had healed a failed human situation. Yet he had been "disfellowshiped" (ecclesiastical foofaraw meaning he was kicked out of his church).

Even if the first marriage was a typically heedless blunder of youth, must this man pay a lifelong penalty for failing to see what no one in either family had seen? The prohibition preventing his return to the Christian community makes it impossible for the church to show compassion. "One finds it difficult to believe that the refusal of compassion reflects the image of Jesus," says biblical scholar John McKenzie. "It seems to put things before people."[9] As the soft heads and hard hearts of the religious moguls prevail, the guest list for the banquet shrinks, and the number of empty chairs at the Lord's table grows. Jesus told us to go out to the highways and byways and drag in the beggars, the cripples, and the broken-hearted; instead, we tell those already seated at the supper table to get up and leave, and we shut the door after them!

John McKenzie, whose writings have exerted a decisive influence on my pastoral ministry, also wrote, "If the church had applied to the texts on divorce the same kind of exegesis it had applied to the more numerous texts on non-violence and the acquisition of wealth, divorce in the Christian community would be no more common than war and riches."[10]

After an exhaustive treatment of the sayings of Jesus prohibiting divorce, Richard B. Hays, professor of New Testament studies at Duke University Divinity School, comments, "Indeed, if one purpose of marriage is to serve as a sign of God's love in the world (by symbolizing the relationship between Christ and the church), how can we reject the possibility that a second marriage after a divorce could serve as a sign of grace and redemption from the sin and brokenness of the past?"

He adds, "No New Testament writer entertains such a suggestion, but I offer it here as a constructive theological proposal. One dares to make such a suggestion precisely because the New Testament itself—especially 1 Corinthians 7—invites its readers into a process of constructive reflection and discernment about the issues of divorce and remarriage."[11]

I'm often asked by Gen-Xers, baby boomers, and senior citizens to name the most important book I've read outside the Bible. My answer has been consistent and unequivocal over the years: *On Being a Christian*, by Hans Küng. The German theologian's portrait of the real Jesus (as opposed to the dreamed-up Jesus) has revolutionized my understanding of Christ and the meaning of Christian discipleship. In passionate and beautifully written prose, he states,

> The church of Jesus Christ is a home not only for the morally upright but for the moral failures and for those who for a variety of reasons have not been able to honor denominational teaching. The Church is a healing community proclaiming the Father's indiscriminate love and unconditional grace, offering pardon, reconciliation and salvation to the down-trodden and leaving the judgment to God.
>
> A Church that will not accept the fact that it consists of sinful men and exists for sinful men becomes hardhearted, self-righteous, inhuman. It deserves neither God's mercy nor men's trust. But if a Church with a history of fidelity and infidelity, of knowledge and error, takes seriously the fact that it is only in God's Kingdom that the wheat is separated from the tares, good fish from bad, sheep from goats, a holiness will be acknowledged in it by grace which it cannot create for itself.

Such a Church is then aware that it has no need to present a spectacle of higher morality to society, as if everything in it were ordered to the best. It is aware that its
faith is weak, its knowledge dim, its profession of faith
halting, that there is not a single sin or failing which it
has not in one way or another been guilty of. And
though it is true that the Church must always dissociate
itself from sin, *it can never have any excuse for keeping any sinners at a distance.* If the Church self-righteously remains
aloof from failures, irreligious and immoral people, it
cannot enter justified into God's kingdom. But if it is
constantly aware of its guilt and sin, it can live in joyous
awareness of forgiveness. The promise has been given to
it that anyone who humbles himself will be exalted.[12]

What to do? Allow me to make a bold biblical suggestion:
Let the church declare a jubilee year in the spirit of the
Book of Leviticus and host a homecoming celebration for all
disenfranchised Christians! In ancient Israel, every seventh, or
"sabbatical," year all debts had to be cancelled; every fiftieth,
or "jubilee," year everything that had been lost was restored to
its original owner and everyone was called to return to his
own home. "In this year of jubilee each of you is to return to
his ancestral home" (Lev. 25:13). In the sabbatical year "you
must permit the land to be redeemed . . . but if he does not
acquire sufficient means to buy back his land, what he has
sold shall remain in the possession of the purchaser until the
jubilee, when it must be released and returned to its original
owner" (Lev. 25:24, 28).

In a year of jubilation that echoes with the joy of the gospel, let the leaders of our churches proclaim amnesty—unconditional, gratuitous pardon for those outside the law; let Jesus' ministry of setting ragamuffins free from shame, humiliation, rejection, and self-hatred be continued; in a magnificent gesture of mercy, let the face of a compassionate God be revealed.

As we have seen, Jesus vindicates his table-companionship with sinners and justifies his revolutionary conduct to his critics by claiming that God's love to the returning sinner knows no bounds. "What I do in word and deed," he says, "represents God's nature and will. . . . Jesus thus claims that in his actions the love of God to the repentant sinner is made effectual."[13] Jesus, by taking sinners into fellowship with *him*, takes them into fellowship with *God*. The awareness that God is love continues to be the ultimate reality for Jesus, and it is the basis for his unprecedented socializing with ragamuffins. This has important implications for the worshiping life of the Christian community.

The transcendence of God is the underlying presupposition of Jesus' preaching and the natural overflowing of his own interior life. The classic definition of preaching remains: *aliis contemplata tradere*—to hand on to others the fruits of one's own contemplation. Père Sertillanges hints at this when he writes,

Let us try to analyze as well as we can the prayer of the Master. To what do his sentiments correspond? What outbursts of soul do they excite? Undoubtedly the first is adoration. . . . [T]o adore is to recognize the whole of the object and the nothingness of the adorer. . . . Adoration is nonentity swooning away and gladly expiring in the presence of Infinity. And that is what Jesus does. He acknowledges that the creature is nothing, nothing but a breath from the divine mouth. He recognizes that He Himself is nothing from the standpoint of that humanity which He animates, marvelous as it is. "Why do you call me good?" He said one day to a young man who had addressed Him as good master. "Only one is good: God." One alone is also great; and the human Christ, with all His glory, is but a ray broken loose from God. By adoration then, He reascended humbly toward His source.[14]

This consciousness of the Father's awesome holiness, total otherness, and mysterious greatness fires Jesus' diatribes against the Pharisees who had presumed to box God in Torah and figure him out in Talmud. However, Jesus' dominant awareness of God is not in terms of power, knowledge, beauty, or otherness; it is in terms of love. Naming God reveals what is new in Jesus' understanding of God: God is close to humankind in love. Hence, the privileged path for gaining access to God is love.

Sunday worship is a public, communal expression of the love of God and neighbor; any cultic action that stands in the way of love stands in the way of God himself. Every celebration of praise and thanksgiving is meant to achieve what Jesus effected in table-fellowship—thanksgiving, peace, mutual acceptance,

reconciliation, fraternity. When worshiping communities continue to harbor grudges and nurture resentments against one
another, when cool cordiality and polite indifference flourish,
when cliques and splinter groups abound and the lines of social,
religious, and ethnic divisions are reinforced, their worship ser-
vices shore up rather than tear down the barriers that divide
people and diminish the quality of life. Communion is celebrated unworthily.

"Worship, cult and religion in general have no absolute
autonomy of their own for Jesus," writes Latin American theologian Jon Sobrino. "His God is not an egocentric being. He
is a being for others, not a being for himself alone. Cultic
worship is not only hypocritical but absolutely meaningless if
it is not accompanied by love for other people; for in such a
case it cannot possibly be a way of corresponding to God."[15]

At a cocktail party in the Midwest, six couples were standing in a circle sipping martinis. One husband turned to his
wife and said, "You're getting so fat that I'm embarrassed to
take you out anymore." What she heard was "I don't love you
anymore." The husband is an elder in his parish and was emu-
lated as a model Christian. But by whose standards? According to Jesus' reply to the lawyer in Matthew 22, the only norm
for a good and faithful disciple is that he be a professional
lover of God and people. Nothing at all can be set in opposi-
tion to right relationships between human beings.

Jesus cuts to the chase: "So then, if you are bringing your
offering to the altar and there remember that your brother has
something against you, leave your offering there before the
altar, go and be reconciled with your brother first, and then

come back and present your offering" (Matt. 5:23–24). What a terrifying reversal of religious priorities! The worship of God and the time of cult are subordinated to reconciliation with one's brother; the value of community worship in the sight of God—independent of the caliber of the music, the effectiveness of the preaching, and the imaginative design of the banners—is measured by the quality of life and love in the community of faith. This Word of God could be as scandalous to the devout Christian as was Jesus' table-fellowship with sinners to the devout Jew.

What enormous potential for healing lies within the worshiping community! If what was said earlier is true—that we can experience the compassion and unconditional acceptance of Jesus Christ only when we feel valued and cherished by others—then it is the church family itself that effects the healing of self-hatred for divorced folks, drunks, scalawags, and social misfits burdened with emotional and mental disorders. The quality of a Christian's presence in the assembly—his relationship not only to God but to his brothers and sisters—is what Paul meant by "recognizing the Body." The Christian's warmth and congeniality, nonjudgmental attitude, and welcoming love may well be the catalyst allowing the healing power of Jesus to become operative in the life of an alienated, forlorn brother or sister. This winsome wedding of worship and life ritualizes Jesus' table-fellowship with sinners and brings healing and wholeness to the entire community.

A GLIMPSE OF JESUS

NOTES

1. Marcus Borg, *Meeting Jesus Again for the First Time* (San Francisco: HarperSanFrancisco, 1994), p. 55.

2. Borg, *Meeting Jesus Again for the First Time*, p. 55.

3. Albert Nolan, O.P., *Jesus Before Christianity* (Maryknoll, NY: Orbis Books, 1976), p. 39.

4. Karl Rahner, *Prayers for a Lifetime* (New York: Crossroad, 1995), p. 23.

5. John F. O'Grady, *Jesus, Lord and Christ* (New York: Paulist Press, 1973), p. 81.

6. Nolan, *Jesus Before Christianity*, p. 38.

7. Hans Küng, *On Being a Christian* (New York: Doubleday, 1976), p. 273.

8. James Gaffney, *Newness of Life: A Modern Introduction to Catholic Ethics* (New York: Paulist Press, 1979), p. 256.

9. John McKenzie, *The New Testament Without Illusion* (Chicago: Thomas More Press, 1980), p. 155.

10. John McKenzie, *What the Bible Says About the Problems of Contemporary Life* (Chicago: Thomas More Press, 1984), pp. 45–46.

11. Richard B. Hays, *The Moral Vision of the New Testament* (San Francisco: HarperSanFrancisco, 1996), p. 373.

12. Küng, *On Being a Christian*, pp. 507–508, italics added.

13. Joachim Jeremias, *The Parables of Jesus* (New York: Scribner, 1970), p. 132.

14. A. D. Sertillanges, *Jesus* (Denville, NJ: Dimension Books, 1976), p. 36.

15. Jon Sobrino, S.J., *Christology at the Crossroads: A Latin American Approach* (Maryknoll, NY: Orbis Books, 1978), p. 167.

4

DELIVERANCE THROUGH STORYTELLING

The eleventh step of the AA program reads: "Sought to improve my conscious contact with God, as I understand him through prayer and meditation, seeking only the knowledge of his will for us and the power to carry it out." After delivering what I considered to be a dazzling explanation of this step—an interpretation filled with profound theological, spiritual, and metaphysical insights—a woman at the meeting approached me and said, "I loved your story about the strawberry." "Yuck," says I. "Ugh," says she. Silently, we nodded in clandestine agreement that one humble strawberry had more power than all my pompous inanities.

There is an extraordinary power in storytelling that stirs the imagination and makes an indelible impression on the mind. Journalist and Christian apologist Malcolm Muggeridge overstates his case to make this point:

Only mystics, clowns and artists, in my experience, speak the truth, which, as Blake keeps insisting, is perceptible to the imagination rather than the mind. Our knowledge of Jesus Christ is far too serious a business to be left to theologians and exegetes alone. From the Middle Ages these professionals have monotonously neglected art and the imagination as guides to religious truth. I find myself in complete agreement with those who wish to reinstate the mystics, clowns and artists alongside the scholars. The imaginable is the believable. To modify Wittgenstein: What we cannot imagine, we must confine to silence and non-belief.[1]

To move through the language and imagery of Jesus' parables offers some fascinating insights into his sensibilities. Noah Webster defines an iconoclast as "one who makes attacks on cherished beliefs and institutions, one who destroys or opposes the veneration of religious images." Jesus, the master storyteller, was clearly an iconoclast. His parables expressed in words what his actions demonstrated. He shattered idols and blew away preconceived ideas of who God is and what men and women are meant to be.

The parables of divine mercy—especially those about a lost coin, a lost sheep, and a lost son—are rooted in Jesus' own experience of his Father. In these parables and others, Jesus speaks wholly and entirely in the light of this reality. The stories were intended, not only to defend his own notorious conduct with sinners, but to startle his critics and stand them on their heads by cracking through their conventional way of thinking about God. Jesus challenged the one-dimensionality of the Pharisees, who gleefully anticipated a day of wrath from which they would be spared because of their orthodoxy and unfaltering piety. Deeply offended by the gospel of reprieve for the wretched, they excoriated Jesus as an irreligious man who did not walk in God's way.

Jesus skewered his opponents, saying in effect,

> The harlots who have no imagined righteousness to pro-tect will be dancing into the Kingdom while you have your alleged virtue burned out of you! Hear me well: I have come to announce the dawn of a new age, an era of incredible generosity. Allow yourselves to be captivated by joy and wonder at the surpassing greatness of my Father's love for the lost; set its life grounded against your own joyless, loveless, thankless, and self-righteous lives. Let go of your impoverished understanding of God and your circumscribed notion of morality. Strike out in a new direction. Cease your loveless ways and be compassionate. Celebrate the homecoming of the lost and rejoice in my Father's munificence.

Here, there is more than deliverance from self-hatred awaiting the Christian who interiorizes and appropriates to himself the meaning of these three parables of the Master. There is holiness as well. "To be a disciple, and thus different from the unconverted pagan, means being as the heavenly Father is: perfect," writes Scripture scholar Donald Senior. "Luke uses the word 'merciful' (6:36). Both terms can be reduced to the same reality. For 'perfect' in Matthew's context means 'whole, complete.' To be whole or complete, as the

Father is complete, means loving with limitless compassion. . . . Following Jesus in his ministry of compassion defines the meaning of 'being perfect as your heavenly Father is perfect.'"[2]

These parables of the Storyteller do not simply shine; they burn. They force us to rethink our faith, get in touch with the God of our own interiority, and reexamine our attitudes toward self and others. Their earthy imagery and language have such a hypnotic appeal to the imagination that they force us to think about them. A sense of foreboding slowly surfaces. Is this Good News too good to be true? Do I want to throw in with the Nazarene? Who is this Storyteller anyway? Is Yahweh actually revealing himself to me in this teller of parables? Is God's mercy in fact manifested in a definitive and decisive way through Jesus of Nazareth?

Besides, what kind of lunatic justice is this that gives preferential treatment to a shiftless bum over his hardworking, nose-to-the-grindstone brother? And that other story he told about the guys who worked only an hour and got the same pay as those who had put in an eight-hour day. Is that fair play? And how about that Samaritan weirdo? I'm not against lending a helping hand, but the wacko do-gooder really overdid it. Helping a man who's been mugged out of the gutter is one thing, but putting him up in a motel and picking up the tab for his room and meals? There goes my beer money for the month! But the real bummer is the one about the butler who went to the slammer because he wouldn't let the maid off the hook for three lousy bucks!

The Storyteller unsettles us. His parables bluntly question our traditional image of God, challenge our invulnerable standards on rectitude and justice, and open up the possibility of a radically new lifestyle that stands in stark contrast to our conventional behavior. Jesus confronts us with a choice: embrace the message disclosed in the parables, or reject it and march to the music of your own drummer. Open up to letting yourself be loved by my Father and living a life of compassion, or return to the regime of secure piety and well-regulated virtue.

Unrelentingly, Jesus stands by his stories and calls out to us for trusting faith, as he did to his Jewish listeners two thousand years ago. Again and again they persisted: "Why do you do this? What makes a prophet associate with riffraff shunned by all respectable people?"

And he replies, "Because they are sick and need me, because they are truly repentant, and because they feel the gratitude of children forgiven by God. Because, on the other hand, you, with your loveless, self-righteous, disobedient hearts, have rejected the gospel. But, above all, because I know what God is like, so good to the poor, so glad when the lost are found, so overflowing with a father's love for the returning child, so merciful to the despairing, the helpless and the needy. That is why!"[3]

Paradoxically, it is another set of stories, known as the "crisis parables"—that Jesus employs to set his people free from the bondage of self-hatred. These parables issue a cry of warning, a summons to repentance because of the lateness of the hour. Jesus says, in effect, "You are having a hurricane party and the tidal wave is approaching. . . . You are feasting and dancing—on the volcano which may erupt at any moment."[4] The impending crisis precludes procrastination. In a variety of similes, the Master says, "Stay awake, because you do not know when the master of the house is coming, evening, midnight, cockcrow, dawn; if he comes unexpectedly, he must not find you asleep. And what I say to you I say to all: 'Stay awake!'" (Matt. 14:33–37).

The implication of Luke 12:35–40 is unmistakable: "See to it that you are dressed for action and have your lamps lit. Be like men awaiting their master to return from a wedding feast. Happy those servants whom the master finds awake when he comes. . . . You too must stand ready, because the Son of Man is coming at an hour you do not expect."

In the parable of the wedding feast (Matt. 22:1–14), the guest without a wedding garment is forcibly seized by the bouncers and heaved out the door. "The festal garment is repentance. Put it on today before your death, the day before the Deluge breaks, put it on today! The demand of the crisis is conversion."[5]

Rome is burning, Jesus says. Drop your fiddle, change your life, and come to me. Let go of nostalgia and mourning for the good old days that never were anyway. A Sunday school in which you never participated, traditional virtues you never practiced, legalistic obedience you never honored, and a sterile orthodoxy you never accepted. The old era is done. The decisive inbreak of God has happened.

The Christian who realizes the gravity of his situation knows that the decision brooks no delay. The Storyteller calls us not to fear but to action. Procrastination only prolongs self-hatred. We cling to cheap, painted fragments of glass when the pearl of great price is being offered to us. When a disciple's very existence is threatened, when he stands on the threshold of moral ruin, when everything is at stake, the hour has struck for bold and resolute decision making. It is not just another itinerant salesperson at the door with superfluous bric-a-brac; it is the Christ of God offering an incredible opportunity, the chance of a lifetime. "I, the light, have come into the world, so that whoever believes in me need not stay in the dark anymore" (John 12:46).

In the parable of the talents, the three servants are called to render an account of how they have used the gifts entrusted to them. The first two servants used their talents boldly and resourcefully. The third, who prudently wrapped up his money and buried it, typifies the Christian who deposits his faith in a hermetic container and seals the lid shut. He limps through life on his grade school catechism and resolutely refuses the challenge of growth and spiritual maturity. He wants to take no risks. But precisely because of this, he loses the gift entrusted to him. "The master wanted his servants to take risks. He wanted them to gamble with his money," says writer/theologian Simon Tugwell.[6]

In a parable (Luke 16:1–8) that was undeniably offensive and provocative to his Jewish audience, Jesus told the story of the crafty steward. We are presented with an embezzler who, to cover his tracks, "cooks the books" by falsifying his employer's accounts. And Jesus praises the criminal!

There was a rich man and he had a steward who was denounced to him for being wasteful with his property. He called for the man and said, "What is this I hear about you? Draw me an account of your stewardship because you are not to be my steward any longer." Then the steward said to himself, "Now that my master is taking the stewardship from me, what I am to do? Dig? I am not strong enough. Go begging? I should be too ashamed. Ah, I know what I will do to make sure that when I am dismissed from office, there will be some to welcome me into their homes."

Then he called his master's debtors one by one. To the first he said, "How much do you owe my master?" "One hundred measures of oil" was the reply. The steward said, "Here, take your bond; sit down straight away and write fifty." To another he said, "And you, sir, how much do you owe?" "One hundred measures of wheat" was the reply. The steward said, "Here, take your bond and write eighty."

The master praised the dishonest steward for his astuteness. For the children of this world are more astute in dealing with their own kind than are the children of light.

The crafty steward is praised not for his dishonesty but for his astuteness. Jesus does not excuse his action but admires his initiative. He did not let a tragic sequence of events destroy him; instead, he did what he had to do, however unscrupulously, to make a new life for himself. Without illusions, he made the most of the little time that remained.

Theologian John Shea comments incisively,

The unjust steward who, hearing he is going to be fired, doctors his master's accounts to secure another job is commended precisely because he acted. The point does not concern morality but apathy. Here is a man who finds himself in a crisis and, instead of wallowing in self-pity, acts resourcefully. The guests who do not respond to the King's banquet are quickly rejected and others are summoned. Immediate response is the mood of the Kingdom. Imaginative shock issues an invitation which leads to decision and action.[7]

The tendency to procrastinate is so prevalent in human beings that it can properly be called an integral part of the human condition. We postpone a decision (which is a decision itself) hoping that the Storyteller will grow weary of waiting and that the imperious inner voice will get laryngitis. The call of the parables remains suspended in a state of floating anxiety so long as we opt neither for nor against the new dimension of living opened up to us. Endless delay creates more problems than it solves and raises again the ominous specter of self-hatred.

Procrastination means that we stop growing for an undetermined length of time; we get stuck. And with the paralysis of analysis, the human spirit begins to shrivel. The conscious awareness of our resistance to grace and the refusal to become who we really are brings a sense of oppression. Our lives become fragmented, inconsistent, lacking in harmony, and out of sync. The worm turns. The apparent security of staying fixed in a familiar place vanishes. Secretly we long for self-transcendence, for a generosity that would lift us above ourselves. We are caught between a rock and a hard place.

How do we resolve this conundrum? We don't. "Perhaps the best that we can say is that while we cannot will ourselves to grace, we can, by will, open ourselves to its miraculous coming. We can prepare ourselves to be fertile ground, a welcoming place."[8] There are no magic words, precise formulas, or esoteric rites of passage to the grace of self-surrender. Only Jesus Christ delivers us from indecision. The Scriptures offer no other basis for ongoing conversion than the personal magnetism of the Master.

Like any good teacher, Jesus frequently repeats himself. He never tires of speaking of the quality of life in the Kingdom and the surpassing joy of the reign of God:

"The kingdom of heaven is like a treasure hidden in a field which someone has found. He hides it again, goes off happy, sells everything he owns and buys the field. Again the kingdom of heaven is like a merchant looking for fine pearls; when he finds one of great value he goes and sells everything he owns and buys it" (Matt. 13:44–46).

The emphasis in these parables, as Joachim Jeremias insists, is neither the cost of discipleship nor a heartless call to heroic action. The twin stories focus on two unmistakable elements: the joy and the delight of discovering the Kingdom of God. If you were notified tomorrow that you had just won the Powerball lottery—three million dollars per year for the next twenty years—there would be no mumbling, grumbling, or complaining about the cruel vicissitudes of life. The only natural response would be sheer delight, delirious joy at the intoxicating prospect of a whole new way of life. Likewise, the treasure-tracker and the pearl-finder bubble with happiness over their serendipitous stroke of fortune. As Joachim Jeremias notes,

> When that great joy, surpassing all measure, seizes a man, it carries him away, penetrates his inmost being, subjugates his mind. All else seems valueless compared with that surpassing worth. No price is too great to pay. The unreserved surrender of what is most valuable becomes a matter of course. The decisive thing in the twin parables is not what the two men give up, but their reason for doing so; the overwhelming experience of the splendor of their discovery. Thus it is with the Kingdom of God. The effect of the joyful news is overpowering; it fills the heart with gladness; it makes life's whole aim the consummation of the divine community and produces the most whole-hearted self-sacrifice.[9]

Nevertheless, our own human experience tells us that the Christian life is not lived to a lyrical beat. Precious and few are those moments of boundless delight and delirious joy. Our personal response to the Storyteller is often halting and half-hearted at best. Because the mystery of iniquity lurks on the landscape and the power of sin waxes strong within us, we may come to the Lord bucking, screaming, and kicking. The self dies a slow death; the resistance to the Spirit remains real. The readiness to relinquish everything is more a painful process than a mystical zap. "We are accustomed to imagining the experience of conversion or sudden call to grace as an 'Oh, joy!' phenomenon," writes Scott Peck. "In my experience, . . . at the moment we finally listen to the call we may say, 'O thank you, Lord'; or we may say, 'O Lord, I am not worthy'; or we may say, 'O shit, do I have to?'"[10]

Yet how often have we heard a person say, "Once I finally made up my mind, I found peace." Jesus, who flinched, talked back to, and questioned his Abba, but still remained faithful, reads the human heart and fully understands the nagging uneasiness and subtle self-hatred induced by procrastination. The Storyteller aims to set us free from fence-straddling through the re-telling of the crisis parables.

Perhaps their spirit can be illustrated by a story of my own:

Once there was a lawyer named Christopher who lived in Jericho, Long Island. When offered the opportunity of a lucrative partnership in Jerusalem, Pennsylvania, he accepted. Uprooting and transplanting the family was a delicate matter. Two of the children were still in high school, and the youngest was in the third grade. Nonetheless, career advancement, prestige, higher income, and a lower cost of living beckoned compellingly. Besides, Christopher reasoned, this would be a new beginning. He could start all over.

How badly he wanted that. His drinking was now out of control. The blackouts, the morning bracer, and the solitary drinking had cunningly crept into his life—almost involuntarily, he felt. How many nights had he slept on the cot in the office after having what he sardonically called "a drink"—a thirty-two-ounce bottle of scotch. His temper tantrums with his secretary were inexcusable. He knew that. Still, it was the pain in Katie's eyes that brought tears to his own. He knew that his wife loved him, but to learn that she had gone to an Alanon meeting last night . . . ?

Well, all that was behind him. Jerusalem would mark the end of the heyday of the booze, the binges, and the bad blood. Jesus, he recalled, had done some memorable things in the biblical town of the same name. So would he.

Christopher did not know that he was destined to spiritual death in Jerusalem.

The family moved, and he stopped drinking. Cold turkey. The withdrawal was excruciating—nausea, vomiting, diarrhea, twitching, hallucinations, and finally convulsions. Katie saved his life that night. Her husband was a man of exquisite sensitivity and fierce independence—a combustible combination that allowed him to defeat John Barleycorn with an iron fist in a velvet glove. All it took was *willpower*, he daily reminded himself. Six weeks of abstinence followed—forty-two full days.

Then his senior partner absconded with the funds, certificates, and stocks—bell, book, and candle. The law firm collapsed in bankruptcy. Christopher regrouped with a double scotch straight up. The physical compulsion and mental obsession returned with a fury.

The next two months were unadulterated hell. The children withdrew, Katie cried herself to sleep, and Christopher routinely drank himself into oblivion. His lights were out, his clock was cleaned, and there was mourning and wailing throughout Jerusalem.

On a Wednesday morning Katie said, "Chris, don't forget your appointment at noon."

He looked up blankly from the newspaper. "What appointment?"

"Remember, you called Alcoholics Anonymous last night and asked for help."

"Like hell I did!" Another blackout. He remembered Peter Jennings on the evening news, but after that. . . .

The doorbell rang; Katie opened the door.

"I'm Harvey from AA," he said. "Your husband called."

Chris escaped into the kitchen. Katie pursued. "Honey, what do you have to lose? Talk with the man."

Grabbing a beer from the refrigerator, Christopher walked into the living room. "Yes? What would you like to talk about?" he asked icily.

"If you put down that can, I'd like to propose a new way of life to you."

For the next two hours Christopher endured the drunkalogue as Harvey shared what his life as an alcoholic used to be like, what happened, and what it was like now. Grudgingly Christopher identified with much of the story. But finally he said, "Thank you, Harvey. I appreciate what you have had to say. My wife is right: I've been abusing the gift of the grape. I'll start today to cut down." And with that, Christopher showed his guest out, vowed to himself that he would not take another drink until eight that evening.

Sipping slowly and triumphantly on his long-awaited scotch, he overheard his wife and eight-year-old son talking in the bedroom. "Vince, why don't you and the other kids play in the pool anymore?"

The boy hesitated. "I guess I'm frightened. I never know

what Dad will be like, and I don't want the other boys to see him drunk."

Hearing those words from his own son was like being stabbed in the heart. The pain of Vince's condemnation sent Christopher's drink crashing to the floor. Tears cascaded down his cheeks, "Christ, what am I doing? What am I missing?"

Christopher arose from his chair and walked out the door into a new way of life.

Jesus comes to us in the Harveys of our lives, in the destructiveness of the prevailing situation, and calls us from despair to hope, from slavery to freedom, from devastating ordinariness to a new way of life. His parables are gifts, shattering our complacency, opening up undreamed-of possibilities, promising that we shall have life and have it in abundance. The imaginative shock of his stories makes theology, by comparison, a dreary screed of abstractions with the leaden tone of an encyclical.

In our cynical, disillusioned world, we may ask, Is this promise of a new way of life merely an illusion, a figment of the imagination? Absolutely not. Let us make a critical distinction: illusion is a denial of reality, while imagination creates and calls forth new reality that has not yet come to birth.

NOTES

1. Quoted in Gerald O'Collins, S.J., *What Are They Saying About Jesus?* (New York: Paulist Press, 1977), p. 61.

2. Donald Senior, C.P., *Jesus: A Gospel Portrait* (Cincinnati: Pflaum Standard, 1975), p. 104.

3.   Joachim Jeremias, *The Parables of Jesus* (New York: Scribner, 1970), p. 146.

4.   Jeremias, *The Parables of Jesus*, p. 163.

5.   Jeremias, *The Parables of Jesus*, p. 188.

6.   Simon Tugwell, *The Beatitudes: Soundings in Christian Traditions* (Springfield, IL: Templegate Publishers, 1980), p. 23.

7.   John Shea, *Stories of God* (Chicago: Thomas More Press, 1978), p. 187.

8.   M. Scott Peck, *The Road Less Traveled* (New York: Simon & Schuster, 1978), p. 308.

9.   Jeremias, *The Parables of Jesus*, p. 201.

10.   Peck, *The Road Less Traveled*, p. 305.

❧ 5 ❧

LIBERATION
THROUGH PRAYER

Whatever else it may be, prayer is first and foremost an act of love. Before any pragmatic, utilitarian, or altruistic motivations, prayer is born of a desire to be with Jesus. His incomparable wisdom, compelling beauty, irresistible goodness, and unrestricted love lure us into the quiet of our hearts where he dwells. To really love someone implies a natural longing for presence and intimate communion.

A saint might be simply defined as an extravagant lover of God and people. In the Catholic church, the first investigation in the canonization process seeks to establish whether the candidate lived a life of *extraordinary* prayer. Although that process has become politicized in unprecedented fashion recently,[1] prayer remains central: the canonization is dismissed and the candidate disqualified—miraculous works, charismatic gifts, and national or worldwide evangelical impact notwithstanding—if the criterion of extravagant love of God manifested through a life of heroic prayer cannot be verified.

Jesus prayed primarily because he loved his Father. Praise, adoration, thanksgiving, intercession, and petition emanated from his profound consciousness of being bonded to the transcendent God in filial intimacy. His personal experience of Yahweh Sabaoth as loving Father shaped not only his self-understanding but, like a knife slashing through wallpaper, brought a dramatic breakthrough into undreamed-of intimacy with God in prayer. Childlike candor, boundless trust, easy familiarity, deep reverence, joyful dependence, unflagging obedience, unmistakable tenderness, and an innate sense of belonging characterized Jesus' prayer.

Trappist monk Basil Pennington captures this simplicity when he writes,

A father is delighted when his little one, leaving off his toys and friends, runs to him and climbs into his arms. As he holds his little one close to him, he cares little whether the child is looking around, his attention flitting from one thing to another, or if he is intent upon his father, or just settling down to sleep. Essentially the child is choosing to be with his father, confident of the love, the care, the security, that is his in those arms. Our Centering Prayer is much like that. We settle down in our Father's arms, in his loving hands. Our mind, our thoughts, our imagination may flit about here and there; we might even fall asleep; but essentially we are choosing to remain for this time intimately with our Father, giving ourselves to him, receiving his love and care, letting him enjoy us as he will. It is very simple prayer. It is very childlike prayer. It is prayer that opens out to us all the delights of the Kingdom.[2]

Through water and the spirit the disciple of Jesus has been bonded to his elder Brother, has entered into God's family, has become a son of the new Covenant, and has been given immediate access to the Father's lap. "Blessed be the God and Father of our Lord Jesus Christ. . . . Before the world was made, he chose us in Christ, to be holy and spotless, and to live through love in his presence, determining that we should become his adopted sons, through Jesus Christ" (Eph. 1:3–4).

The problem is: either we do not know it, we know it but do not accept it; we accept it but are not in touch with it; we are in touch with it but do not surrender to it.

Self-hatred is not a spiritual sickness that I divined to justify the writing of another book. In my pastoral experience, it is the dominant malaise crippling Christian people and stifling their growth in the Holy Spirit. Psychiatrist friends in Seattle and Louisville, New York and Los Angeles, have shared with me the pandemic of clients tormented by intense feelings of guilt, shame, remorse, and self-punishment.

The melancholy spirit of Chekhov's plays—"You are living badly, my friend"—haunts the American conscience. The disparity between our ideal and our real self; the grim specter of past infidelities; the awareness that I am not living what I believe, that I am not all I ought to be, that I am not measuring up to others' expectations regarding demeanor and lifestyle; the relentless pressure of conformity; the midlife oppression of what I had hoped to become versus what I have actually become; the obsession with personal dishonesty and self-centeredness; and the mournful nostalgia for *The Blue Lagoon* combine to transform an expectant pilgrim people into a dispirited traveling troupe of brooding Hamlets, frightened Rullers, and wiped-out Willy Lomans. Alcoholism, workaholism, mounting addictive behaviors across the board, and an alarming suicide rate indicate the magnitude of the problem.

In our struggle with self-hatred, we obviously do not like what we see. We find it uncomfortable, if not intolerable, to confront our true selves; and so, like runaway slaves, we either flee our own reality or manufacture a false self—mostly admirable, mildly prepossessing, and superficially happy. Defense mechanisms become useful allies here. These unconscious ploys warp our perception of reality and protect us from fear, loss, and emotional pain. Through the smokescreen of rationalization, projection, displacement, insulation, intellectualization, and generalization, we remain on the merry-go-round of denial and dishonesty. Those of us who have played this game wear a thousand masks to disguise the face of fear.

The incomparable Henri Nouwen wrote,

There is so much fear in us. Fear of people, fear of God and much raw, undefined, free-floating anxiety. I wonder if fear is not our main obstacle to prayer. When we enter into the presence of God and start to sense the huge reservoir of fear in us, we want to run away into the many distractions which our busy world offers so abundantly. But we should not be afraid of our fears. We can confront them, give words to them and lead them into the pres-

ence of him who says, "Do not be afraid, it is I." Our incli-
nation is to show the Lord only what we are comfortable
with. But the more we dare to reveal our whole trembling
self to him, the more we will be able to sense that his
love, which is perfect love, casts out all our fears.[3]

To pray is to "return to ourselves," where God dwells, and
to accept ownership of our sinfulness, poverty, and powerless-
ness. Only when the prodigal son returned to himself and
took inventory of his desperate plight did he begin the journey home to his father. "One of the reasons why our meditation never gets started," wrote the late Thomas Merton, "is
that perhaps we never make this real, serious return to the
center of our own nothingness before God. Hence we never
enter into the deepest reality of our relationship with him."[4]

The Lord hears the cry of the poor. When the armistice
with self-hatred is signed and we embrace what we really are,
the process of liberation begins. But so often we are afraid to
initiate the process for fear of rejection. Feeling like Quasi-
modo (the hunchback of Notre Dame), we daub cosmetics
and spiritual makeup on our misery and supposed ugliness to
make ourselves appear presentable to God. This is not our
true self. Authentic prayer calls us to rigorous honesty, to
come out of hiding, to quit trying to seem impressive, to
acknowledge our total dependence on God and the reality of
our sinful situation. It is a moment of truth when defenses fall
and the masks drop in an instinctive act of humility.

This eleventh-hour opening of consciousness has been
observed in mental hospitals where mute patients, faced with

the reality of the impending showdown, have suddenly begun to speak with passionate conviction about their lives. The prospect of impending death has loosened their tongues in the urgent awareness that, having lost so much already, they have nothing further to lose through repression and silence.

Jesus says, "Blessed are those who know that they are poor" (Matt. 5:3, NEB). We must know who we are. How difficult it is to be honest—to accept that I am unacceptable, to renounce self-justification, to give up my preposterous pretending that my paltry prayers, spiritual insights, knowledge of Scripture, and blustering successes in ministry have made me pleasing to God. No antecedent beauty enamors me in his eyes. I am lovable because He loves me. Period. The first step in liberation from self-hatred is to move from the darkness of self-delusion into the daylight of God's truth.

"We must learn the art of weakness," writes Simon Tugwell, "of non-achievement, of being able to cope with the knowledge of our own poverty and helplessness without trying to escape from it into something we can accept more easily. And we must know that it is even in that poverty and helplessness that God sees us with love, even with approbation, however much it may be tinged with sadness and censure. God never says to us, 'I want you to be something else' without also saying, 'I love you as you are.'"⁵

The Christ of my interiority calls me back tirelessly and insistently to the primordial truth of his unconditional love. His Good News is proclaimed to what we really are, whether we like it or not. Yet the debilitating effects of personal sin make for monstrous resistance to accepting acceptance. A darkened intellect, a weakened will, and a panoply of jaded emotions are the stony soil into which the Word of God falls.

From years of clinical practice, psychiatrist M. Scott Peck has not only come to believe in original sin, he has given it a precise definition—*laziness*.[6] Prayer becomes a chore rather than a joy. We drag ourselves out of bed for morning praise, shuffle off to Sunday worship with the sacramental slump of the terminally ill, get a reprieve when the pastor dismisses us with "go in peace," and endure the tedium of night prayer with stoic resignation, knowing that "this too shall pass." The Enemy, who specializes in treacherous disguise, is the lazy part of self, resisting the effort, asceticism, and discipline that a serious life of prayer demands. The faulty logic of a darkened intellect permits dubious rationalizations such as, "My work is my prayer," "I am too busy," and "I pray only when I feel a prompting of the Spirit." These lame excuses allow us lazily to maintain the status quo and indefinitely postpone the tryst with unconditional love.

Moreover, the *quid pro quo* character of human love, with its inevitable disillusionments and disappointments, unconsciously becomes operative in the divine encounter and impedes the inbreak into Mystery. The lived experience of gratuitous love that knows no boundary, limit, or breaking point is a *rara avis*, even in honeymoon havens such as Bali H'ai and the Poconos.

But what if it should come to pass?

Again, laziness, manifested as fear of the sweat and struggle involved in spiritual growth, intrudes. God loves me as I am, but will he let me *stay* where I am? Where does the road lead? The dread of journeying into the unknown, the uneasiness of knowing that the Holy One will not be manipulated, that he cannot be conned into granting consolation when he is calling for conversion, that accepting unconditional love leads to loving unconditionally in return—these stumbling blocks discourage every prodigal from returning to himself. Their names are laziness and fear.

Anyone who walks in alcoholic bones is no stranger to self-deception. He steps gingerly through the minefield of dishonesty and deceit, knowing that his very life hangs in the balance. No one has ever intellectualized himself into sobriety (*I* sure as hell haven't), just as no one has ever intellectualized himself into prayer. Recognition of the problem is not the answer. *Action* is. One learns to pray by *praying*.

Two twenty-minute periods of prime time in solitary prayer, morning and evening, before a symbol of the crucified Christ is the most effective discipline I have found for making conscious contact with the living God and his liberating love.

Why the symbol of the crucified Christ? Because it is an icon of the greatest act of love in human history. Lamentably, Christian piety has prettified the passionate God of Golgotha; Christian art has banalized unspeakable outrage into dignified jewelry; Christian worship has sentimentalized monstrous scandal into sacred pageant. We have corrupted our sense of reality by sentimentalizing it. Pious imagination, romantic preaching, and lifeless or raucous worship overshadow the real Jesus. The Christian should tremble and the whole community quake when contemplating the cross on the Friday we call Good. But organized religion has domesticated the crucified Lord of glory into a tame theological symbol. He does not disturb our comfortable piety. Yet all the heretics, terrorists, and flamboyant preachers put together create less havoc than the Crucified when, "instead of remaining an icon, he comes to life and delivers us over to the fire that he came to light."[7]

For the believing Christian, praying with a small cross held in the hand exposes skepticism as academic posturing, cynicism as a loss of nerve, and indifference as downright bad faith. The crucified Christ, in his present risenness, is not an abstraction but the ultimate response to how far love will go, what measure of rejection it will endure, how much infidelity, self-centeredness, and betrayal it will withstand. The unconditional love of Jesus Christ nailed to the wood does not flinch before the worst sinner's perversity and inhumanity. "He took our sicknesses away and carried our diseases for us" (Matt. 8:17).

The Christ of Christian prayer is the Risen One who still bears the nail marks of the earthly Jesus, without which he would not be identical with the Nazarene. Ernst Käsemann does not mince words:

> Harsh though it may sound, it is obvious that Christ is denied today by Christians most of all, because his lordship over their organized religion and their dogmatic convictions has become illusory, theoretical and imaginary. But the token which distinguishes his lordship from the lordship of other religious founders is undoubtedly the cross and the cross alone.[8]

Our presence to Christ in prayer can accomplish nothing of itself, but it does create the situation where he may speak to us through his Spirit if he wishes, enlighten our minds with his wisdom, and liberate us from self-hatred if he deems it opportune.

I'd like to share an exercise that I've found profitable for experiencing the love of Jesus Christ. I learned it from an old evangelical pastor who seemed to have the gift for mediating the experience of Jesus Christ, the risen Lord, to people who asked to come in touch with Christ. As nearly as I can remember the pastor's words, his method was something like this:

Let us suppose a woman came to this pastor and said, "I want to get in touch with the risen Lord." The pastor would lead her to a quiet corner. Taking a seat, they would both close their eyes and bow their heads in prayer.

The pastor would then say something like this to the woman: "Listen carefully to what I have to say now: Jesus Christ, the risen Lord, is present here and now with us. Do you believe this?"

After a pause the woman would say, "Yes, I believe it."

"Now I am going to get you to consider something that is even more difficult to believe. Jesus Christ, the risen Lord who is present here, loves and accepts you just as you are. . . . You do not have to change to get his love. . . . You do not have to become better . . . to get out of your sinful ways. . . . He obviously wants you to become better. He obviously wants you to give up your sin. But you do not have to do this to get his love and acceptance. That you have already, right now, just as you are, even before you decide to change, and whether you decide to change or not. . . . Do you believe

92

this? . . . Take your time over it. . . . Then decide whether you believe it or not."

After some reflection the woman would say, "Yes, I believe that too."

"Well then," the pastor would say, "say something to Jesus. Say it aloud."

The woman would then begin to pray aloud to the Lord— and it wouldn't be long before she grasped the pastor's hand and said, "I know exactly what you mean about experiencing him. He's *here!* I can sense his presence."

Sheer imagination? A special charism given to our good pastor? Perhaps. But the fact is, whether or not this method is adequate for putting a person in contact with the risen Lord, it's certainly a sound one both spiritually and theologically, and the method is certainly conducive to making a person feel the infinite treasures of the love of Christ. Try it for yourself:

Recall the presence of the risen Lord with you. Tell him that you believe that he is present to you.

Reflect on the fact that he loves and accepts you just as you are now. Take time out to sense his unconditional love for you as he looks at you *lovingly* and *humbly.*

Speak to Jesus—or just lovingly stay in silence and communicate with him beyond words.

A soul-deep emphasis on the love of Christ (what the ancients called "devotion to the heart of Jesus"), so vigorous in the past, so much on the decline today, would flourish once again if people would understand that it consists essentially in accepting Jesus Christ as love incarnate, as the manifestation of the unconditional love of God for us. Anyone who accepts this truth is bound to experience fruits *beyond all expectations* in his or her own prayer life and ministry. As Anthony de Mello, considered by many to be a spiritual genius, writes, "The great turning point in your life comes not when you realize that you love God but when you realize and fully accept the fact that God loves you unconditionally."[9]

Alas, neither my seminary training, my forty years in ministry, nor the catastrophic events of 9/11/01 prepared me for the news, but some well-informed sources recently reported that the end of the world is imminent. Though Jesus himself disclaimed any knowledge of the day or the hour (Matt. 24:36), these visionaries have assured us that the nuclear impasse is at the brink, the global village is teetering on the edge, the Twin Towers murders were the portent, and very soon things will be all over for the human adventure.

These seers, clothed in their fictive rags of infallible foresight, may indeed be correct in their apocalyptic ultimatum that human history is coming to an end and the extermination of the species is at hand. The evils of the present generation may indeed be interpreted as signs signaling God's final intervention to bring about the end-time in awesome destruction and incredible triumph. Or they may be totally wrong.

"Apocalyptic holds a certain morbid fascination for the human mind," observes James Mackey. "It easily outlives the circumstances which give it birth, and always finds groups to predict the end of the world over the graves of all former predictions. Symbols are always vulnerable to over-literal minds and the inflated images of apocalyptic seem more prone than most to be taken literally. But the tendency to take apocalyptic too literally is due to a disease of the human mind rather than to any inherent fault in apocalyptic itself. It is due to a failure of nerve, to the hypochondriac's penchant for exaggerating the evils of the age, and to the coward's anxious search for an escape clause in humanity's contract with history."[10]

Whether the end-time is imminent or not, the lordship of Jesus Christ extends over the cosmic continuum. "I am the Alpha and the Omega, the First and the Last, the Beginning and the End" (Rev. 22:13). Authentic prayer puts us in touch with this reality and liberates us from the tyranny of time. Jesus' word calls us to conscientious conduct in the world today; *tomorrow's* survival is *his* responsibility.

The New Testament knows only the linear concept of time. Creation marked the beginning, the death/resurrection of Christ is the decisive midpoint, and his Second Coming determines the end-time. But this latter, future event is no longer the center of redemptive history. Regardless of the precise date of the Parousia, we are living in the last days, or, in theologian Oscar Cullman's oft-quoted phrase, in "the isness of the shall be."[11] The final stage of salvation-history was inaugurated on Easter Sunday.

By way of illustration, many historians see the battle of Iwo Jima as the turning point of World War II in the South Pacific. This decisive victory, so close to the heart of the Japanese mainland, was achieved in March of 1945; yet the war continued for months until VJ Day. Though the significance of the flag-raising on Iwo Jima wasn't fully perceived by all, it nevertheless made eventual conquest of the Japanese inevitable.

In the Christian view of history, the end-time is coming, but the world is already ruled by Christ by virtue of his decisive Easter victory.

Several times a day most of us glance at our watch or the wall clock or ask a colleague, "What time is it?" To our earthbound minds Jesus whispers in prayer,

Now is the time! The "real" world of price tags, designer jeans, Gucci handbags, Monopoly money, the iron umbrella of nuclear deterrence, beaver vests, Persian rugs, silk underwear, and Super Bowl LXXVII is passing away. *Now* is the time to stop running around frantically like Lancelot's horse in four directions at once and quietly remember that only one thing is necessary. *Now* is the time for creative response to my Word and for saving solutions for your brothers and sisters.

Let me tell you a little story:

One year a rich fool had a bonanza crop and made provisions for a yet-heavier one. He said to himself, "You're a good ol' boy. You've worked hard, deserve everything that's coming to you, and have a nest egg for the future. Take it easy, eat heartily, drink up a storm, and have a good time."

That night my Father shattered his security. "Fool!" he said. "This very night the demand will be made for your soul; and this hoard of yours, who is going to enjoy it now?"

In prayer Jesus slows us down to a human tempo, teaches us to count how few days we have, gifts us with wisdom of heart, and liberates us from the oppression of false deadlines, myopic vision, and the degradation of language. (With reference to the latter, I have discovered that prayer has purified my vocabulary of many boring, colorless, puffy, and apparently damned important words like *maximize, prioritize, interact, facilitate, interface, input, feedback,* and *bottomline.* There is a conspicuous absence of empty, overused words in Jesus' speech. We find no trace of impacting, hopefully, at this point in time, parameters, or linkages in the Gospel; in fact, there are no junk words, jargon, or *meaningful* nonsense at all.)

Sir Thomas More, eulogized by playwright Robert Bolt as a "man for all seasons," is my candidate for the patron saint of the twenty-first century. His marvelous sense of humor evolved from his concept of linear time, a lucid, sensible appreciation of death, and the folly of this transitory world. More's life was anchored in Jesus Christ, the Alpha and Omega who rules as Lord over all things in heaven and on earth. In More's worldview it had already been drawn inexorably into the redemptive process. No power or principality could prevail against Christ's lordship over time. God had destined More's world for good, and in spite of the most fearful indications to the contrary, good would triumph because Jesus had already accomplished the victory.

More, a martyr because he refused to take the oath of allegiance to Henry VIII, later saw through the make-believe character of this world and could not stop laughing at human conceit. "So clear was his intuitive vision of the Eternal that he could only see life in this world from God's point of view. So much of what he saw looked so very much like playacting that he could not take it seriously."[12]

Husband, father, prominent statesman, author, and political man of his times (the early 1500s), More was nonetheless a true contemplative who lived an extraordinary life of prayer. "He is, in a sense, the superb example of a man whose sense of humor stemmed from his prayer and mirrored his love of God. Seeing this life as a stage and all the men and women merely players, he could only see the funny side of human conceit."[13]

With notable exceptions, most of the canonized saints seem to be otherworldly and grim, if not downright forbidding. The gaunt ascetic who practices heroic self-denial may seem to take a dim view of the world and human relationships. The apostolic workaholic may give the impression that he has mislaid true peace and joy. The spartan who is merciless with himself may incline to be unbending with others. Thomas More, *au contraire*, was a charming, delightful, and witty man who was *in* the world and *of* the world, attached to the city and devoted to the temple. His life of prayer preserved that delicate balance in fruitful tension.

In our own era—oversaturated with savvy media working to seduce the human spirit, to persuade us that happiness lies in the swirling caress of an onyx jacuzzi, to insist that "looking good" is everything, and to pontificate that an overnight trip to the Minneapolis mall (our cathedral of consumption) will provide emotional relief, ultimate solace, and a religious experience—More's realism and mordant wit are timely, sobering, and benignly outrageous. His revolt against unreality and his ruthless rejection of humbug put time and its trappings in biblical perspective.

More's most hilarious barbs were reserved for kings and clergy, talkative nuns and inflated theologians, and one Elmer Gantry–like character called Candidus, a parish priest who was a dubious model of Christian discipleship:

> *As a faithful mirror view it,*
> *Showing what to do—what shun;*
> *All he shuns take care to do it,*
> *All he does, take care to shun.*[14]

It would not have been uncharacteristic of More to lampoon contemporary theology in the style of this anonymous wit: "Jesus said to his disciples, 'Who do men say that I am?' And they answered him: 'You are the eschatological manifestation of the ground of our being, in whom we find the ultimate fulfillment in our interpersonal relationships.' And Jesus said: 'What?'"

Yet, for all More's witty and savage attacks on the establishment, his prayer life exerted a decisive influence on his political thought, political passion, and political action. As chancellor of England, More did not run *from* the world but *to* it, in Christ Jesus. He got deeply involved in British trade agreements and labor negotiations, championed the rights of the poor and oppressed who were being used as cattle, waged war on high prices and the shortage of food, bitterly opposed the bellicose political stance of several popes, urged the reform of law and the spread of scholarship, and became so embroiled in his own personal declaration of religious freedom he was martyred at the hands of King Henry VIII in 1535.

Liberated through prayer from the tyranny of time, More could proclaim unpretentiously, "The King's good servant but God's first." His sense of humor did not desert him even on the scaffold. As the executioner raised high the axe, More implored that his beard be spared from the block, "for this has committed no treason."[15]

The patron saint of the American church for the twenty-first century? Why not? In the year 1929, the late G. K. Chesterton prophesied, "Sir Thomas More is more important at this moment than at any moment since his death, even perhaps the great moment of his dying; but he is not quite so important as he will be in a hundred years time."[16]

In Iris Murdoch's thoughtful novel *The Nice and the Good*, a man is caught in a boundary situation: he is trapped in a cave, waist-deep in water, and time is running out. Soon the high tide will inundate the place, leaving no escape. In a moment of great lucidity, he ruminates, "If I ever get out of here, I will be no man's judge, . . . not to judge, not to be superior, not to exercise power, not to seek, seek, seek. All power is sin and all law is frailty. Love is the only justice. Forgiveness, reconciliation, not law."[17]

With time slipping away like sand in an hourglass, the church has no more urgent priority than proclaiming the values of Jesus, preparing the way for him, and restraining panic when he appears on the scene. It is neither bogged down in heresy-hunting nor mired in the ecclesiastical morass of theological controversies. Ignoring every issue that is petty and irrelevant, the Body of Christ must come together in fraternal love, forgive one another for centuries of malfeasance, let people hear and respond to the Master's life-giving question to Peter, "Do you love me?" and allow Jesus' sovereignty to become a reality in the realm of Christian freedom.

The *qahal Yahweh* of the Hebrew Scriptures, the *ekklesia* of the Christian Scriptures and the *holy assembly* of the Koran all call people to renounce mean-minded narrowness and celebrate monotheistic unity, to bond together in little communities that pray together and heal and serve one another, because, as Hans Küng concludes, "the Kingdom of God is a dwelling place for men. What else can it signify but a condition in which human existence is not only tolerable but joyful—because it is open to infinity."[18]

One should not lose sight of this central truth: the earthquake in the life of Thomas More occurred in the purifying solitude of prayer. It was not only a liberating and lacerating revelation but a revolutionary one as well. "Jesus Christ is the same yesterday, today and forever" (Heb. 13:8). Why should the experience of liberation from the dominion of self-hatred and the tyranny of time be any different for us?

NOTES

1.   See Richard McBrien, *Lives of the Saints* (San Francisco: HarperSanFrancisco, 2001), pp. 52–54.

2.   Basil Pennington, O.C.S.O., *Centering Prayer* (Garden City, NY: Doubleday, 1980), pp. 68–69.

3.   Henri J. M. Nouwen, *A Cry for Mercy* (Garden City, NY: Doubleday, 1981), p. 23.

4.   Thomas Merton, *The Climate of Monastic Prayer*, quoted in Pennington, *Centering Prayer*, p. 73.

5.   Simon Tugwell, *The Beatitudes: Soundings in Christian Traditions* (Springfield, IL: Templegate, 1980), p. 15.

6.   M. Scott Peck, *The Road Less Traveled* (New York: Simon & Schuster, 1978), p. 184.

7.   Ernst Käsemann, *Jesus Means Freedom* (Philadelphia: Fortress Press, 1969), p. 150.

8.   Ernst Käsemann, *Perspectives on Paul* (Philadelphia: Fortress Press, 1971), p. 54.

9.   Anthony de Mello, S.J., *Sadhana: A Way to God* (St. Louis: Institute of Jesuit Sources, 1978), pp. 114–116.

10.   James P. Mackey, *Jesus: The Man and the Myth* (New York: Paulist Press, 1979), p. 126.

11.   Oscar Cullman, *Christ and Time* (Philadelphia: Westminster Press, 1956), p. 84. The author's insight into the early Christian conception of time and history is the basis for my reflection.

12.   Bernard Bassett, S.J., *Born for Friendship: The Spirit of Sir Thomas More* (New York: Sheed & Ward, 1965), p. 40.

13.   Bassett, *Born for Friendship*, p. 43.

14.   Bassett, *Born for Friendship*, p. 41.

15.   Bassett, *Born for Friendship*, p. 211.

16.   G. K. Chesterton, *The Fame of Blessed Thomas More* (New York: Sheed & Ward, 1929), p. 63. Quoted by Bassett, foreword to *Born for Friendship*.

17.   Iris Murdoch, *The Nice and the Good* (New York: Penguin Books, 1978), p. 315.

18.   Hans Küng, *On Being a Christian*, p. 324.

6

INTEGRITY AND
SELF-ACCEPTANCE

One sweltering summer morning, when casserole heat baked the Big Easy, four Christians of varying intensity were strolling through the French Quarter. It was a plotted playday, a mischievous escape from the weary round of work. The hour was gliding toward noon. We passed the great jazz emporium, Preservation Hall, browsed in a homely boutique to sniff scented candles, ambled around Jackson Square, and inspected the menu at Pontalba's, featuring red beans and rice. A trifling temptation! We were moving in para-liturgical procession to Central Grocery, home of the original muffuletta sandwich. My face was set like flint, and Paul's eyes narrowed with the apocalyptic glint of an aimed gun. Salivating in greedy anticipation of the first bite—Genoa salami, provolone cheese, diced olives, bologna, and prosciutto, all wedged into a cavernous sesame bun and laced with a bewitching sauce, we sat down at a circular marble table.

Paul turned to me and asked, "What do you want to do with the rest of your life?"

With only slight hesitation I replied, "I would like the epitaph on my tombstone to read, 'Here lies a loving man.'"

Even when preoccupied, distracted, or salivating, we each have a dream, a vision of life that corresponds to our convictions, embodies our uniqueness, and expresses what is lifegiving within us. Whether altruistic or ignoble, the dream gives definition to our lives, influencing the decisions we make, the steps we take, and the words we speak.

If security represents our highest aspiration, we may be owned and indentured by Aetna Life and Casualty; if pleasure is our priority, we will distribute our time and money in hedonistic pursuits; if scholarship rules, we will be properly pedigreed and securely settled in an academic environment. Even if the dream is unrealistic or temporarily on hold due to uncontrollable circumstances, it prods our consciousness, nurtures our fantasies, and inchoately sustains our will-to-meaning in the world.

The dream of Jesus Christ is the Kingdom of God, and the committed Christian buys into his dream.

It ought to be noted that the Kingdom is not an abstraction. It is a concrete, visible, and formidable reality forged by the personal commitment of many members. A commitment that does not issue in humble service, suffering discipleship, and creative love is an illusion. The world has no interest in abstractions, and Jesus Christ is impatient with illusions: "Everyone who listens to these words of mine and does not act on them will be like a stupid man who built his house on sand" (Matt. 7:26).

"The one who talks, especially if he talks to God, can affect a great deal," writes philosopher Maurice Blondel, "but the one who acts really means business and has more claim on our attention. If you want to know what a person really believes, don't listen to what he says but watch what he does."[1]

A life of integrity is born of fidelity to the dream. Daily we make choices that are either consistent with or contrary to the gospel vision. The mature Christian harmoniously integrates her faith, intellect, and feelings in consistent and fairly predictable behavior patterns. The sense of serenity that springs from this internal continuity is self-acceptance. The need for approval and the hunger for human respect diminish in proportion to our integrity. (The Scriptures call it *righteousness*, but the word has a pejorative tone in our times, as does *piety*, and both ought to be scrapped until such time as words are restored to their original meaning. They conjure up notions of legalism, spiritual superiority, and sanctimonious moralism that would make Jesus shudder.)

Each Christian gives flesh and bone to the dream with his/her unique, mysterious, and irreplaceable personality. The Word of God calls into being a faith-community characterized by unity without uniformity. Jesus is the way, but his light is refracted in myriad ways by multiple personalities.

"To be open to the Way, the Truth and the Life, we should find the unique task and expression of divine love Jesus wants in our lives," writes Adrian van Kaam, "in countless loving and caring ways, we can put ourselves in our daily tasks and encounters, but only one way can build the style of divine caring each one of us is uniquely called to by the Lord. There are many tempting possibilities to care in ways that are at odds with the way Christ wants to express care in us. We may try to live a style of love we are not called to. We may want to concretize our care for people in a task or movement not attuned to our individual nature. We may do so to please others because we crave to be liked. Or we may want to belong to a popular social or apostolic movement. We join in blindly in spite of the fact that their particular manifestation of Christ's love is not necessarily ours."[2]

Discerning the direction that the dream should take in our lives requires fidelity to our feelings. Emotions, mistrusted and much maligned in the checkered history of Christian spirituality, are integral parts of our total self. They are the most direct reaction to our perception of ourselves and the world around us. Whether positive or negative, feelings put us in touch with our true selves. They are neither good nor bad; they are simply the truth of what is going on within us. What we do with them determines whether we live lives of honesty or deceit. The familiar reproach, "You lied to me," is often valid even when we have told the truth! The other only heard what we said but not what we meant because we repressed our feelings. When submitted to the discretion of a faith-formed intellect, our emotions serve as accurate and trustworthy beacons for appropriate action or inaction.

Feelings that are not expressed cannot be fixed. For example, suppressed anger leads to resentment; repressed resentment leads to guilty self-flagellation; guilt leads to depression. Repressed persons are often depressed persons. An integral life implies creative listening to our emotions, taking responsibility for them, and courageously expressing them. The denial, displacement, or suppression of feelings constitutes infidelity to the dream and leads to a loss of integrity.

A story is told about five computer saleswomen from Milwaukee who went to a regional sales convention in Chicago. They assured their husbands that they would return in ample time for dinner. The meeting ran over time, and the women raced to the train station tickets in hand. As they barged through the terminal, one woman inadvertently kicked over a table supporting a basket of apples. A ten-year-old boy was selling apples to pay for his books and clothes for school. Without breaking stride, the group clambered aboard the train with a sign of relief. All but one. She paused, got in touch with her feelings, and experienced a twinge of compunction for the kid whose applestand had been overturned. She told her companions that she would catch the next train and returned to the terminal. Later she said, "I'm really glad I did, because the ten-year-old boy was blind."

As the woman gathered up the apples scattered about the floor, she noticed that several were bruised. She reached in her pocket and said to the child, "Please accept twenty dollars for the apples I damaged. I hope I didn't spoil your day. God bless you."

As she started walking away, the bewildered blind boy called after her, asking, "Are you Jesus?"

To ignore, repress, or be inattentive to our feelings is to fail to listen to the stirrings and surprises of the Spirit within our emotional structure calling us to creative response.

Jesus listened. In John's gospel we are told that "he was moved with the deepest emotions" (11:33). In Matthew his anger erupts: "You hypocrites! It was you Isaiah meant when he prophesied: These people honor me only with lip-service, while their hearts are far from me. The worship they offer me is worthless" (15:7–9). He called the crowd to intercessory prayer because "he felt sorry for them because they were harassed and dejected like sheep without a shepherd" (Matt. 9:16). When he saw the widow of Nain, "he felt sorry for her. 'Don't cry,' he said" (Luke 7:13). Would her son have been restored to life if Jesus had repressed his feelings?

Grief, frustration, and sadness all spontaneously broke through when he "drew near and came in sight of [the city], he shed tears for it and said, 'If you in your turn had only understood the message of peace'" (Luke 19:41). There was no trace of emotional restraint when Jesus roared, "You liars! The devil is your father and you prefer to do what your father wants" (John 8:44). When dining at Simon's house in Bethany, there was more than a hint of irritation, as he said of the woman who anointed him with costly nard, "Leave her alone. Why are you upsetting her?" (Mark 14:6). We hear utter frustration in the words "How much longer must I put up with you?" (Matt. 15:17), unmitigated rage in "Get behind me, Satan! You are an obstacle in my path" (Matt. 16:23), extraordinary sensitivity in "Who touched me? I felt that power had gone out from me" (Luke 8:47), and blazing wrath in "Get them out of here! Stop turning my Father's house into a marketplace" (John 2:16).

The gospel portrait of Jesus is that of a man exquisitely attuned to his emotions and uninhibited in expressing them. One finds in Christ no attitude of scorn, contempt, fear, ridicule, or rejection of feelings as being fickle, flaky, and unreliable. They were sensitive emotional antennae to which he listened carefully and through which he perceived the will of his Father for congruent speech and action. (There's an untapped mine of spiritual wisdom in the soporific slogan, "If it feels good, do it." Admittedly, its meaning has been bent, twisted, spindled, and mutilated by Hedonists and Epicureans in order to rationalize licentious behavior. Nevertheless, good feelings, consonant with our faith-commitment and intellectual perception, are signals for creative Christian conduct fruitful for ourselves, others, and the building of the Kingdom.

The light we are seeking is inside. So often we search for God willy-nilly and do not find him until we return to ourselves. In active listening to our feelings we encounter the Holy, not in the earthquake and fire outside but, like Elijah, "in the sound of a gentle breeze" (1 Kings 19:23). The Kingdom of God is in our midst.

Jesus' freedom from public opinion and the nagging concern over what others might think enabled him to vent his emotions with honesty and spontaneity. There could be no facade, no mask, no pretense, no sham, no playing of roles. For the Nazarene carpenter, to have integrity meant to be genuine, to communicate authentically, to resonate with his feelings. On the contrary, to be false, two-faced, to be less than real, to say one thing and mean another was to lose self and deny the dream. "I tell you this, that for every unfounded word men utter they will answer on Judgment Day, since it is by your words you will be acquitted, and by your words condemned" (Matt. 12:36).

A life of integrity is not necessarily a life of conformity. The injunction of Paul to "put on Christ" (Rom. 13:14) explicitly means *not* to conform to the spirit of this passing age. With utter single-mindedness and purity of heart, Jesus sought only to please his Father. He was unconcerned about projecting a "nice guy" image and surely not paranoid about hurting anyone's feelings or stepping on anyone's toes.

"There is a kind of tyranny of public opinion which we often find at work in human life, in our own lives: What will the neighbors think! What will my friends think! What will people think! The expectations of others often act as a subtle but controlling pressure on behavior," writes Manhattan University scholar Donald Gray. "But the claim of God's Kingdom takes precedence over the claims of what others may think, even if that priority is difficult to observe. Because he remains free for the claims of the Kingdom, Jesus is able to maintain a freedom from the narrow judgments of those who would straitjacket him in a conventional mold.[3]

Theologian John Haughey has remarked that the best way for anyone to grow is "to put down roots." Jesus' life reflected a developing consciousness of his person and his mission through rootedness in his Father. Like a massive oak tree with its roots buried deep in the earth, Jesus' heart was buried in the One whom he affectionately called "Abba" and bonded in love in a way that goes beyond our understanding. He clung to his Father and never camouflaged his feelings, shouted with the crowd or rippled in the wind of pusillanimity and compromise. He knew who he was—the Son, Servant, and Beloved of his Father—and he permitted nothing and no one to stand in his way of being himself. "Not the law, not the tradition, not the past, not the authorities, not public opinion, not even death itself," notes Gray. "Nothing! He will be the Father's Son, which is the very essence of his identity. He will be himself."[4]

In the full acceptance of who he was, Jesus is the archetype of personality integration. When we "put on Christ" and fully accept who we are, a healthy independence from peer pressure, people-pleasing, and human respect develops. Christ's preferences and values become our own. The Kingdom of God is built on earth when we do the will of our Father in heaven. We become "other Christs" through a life of Christian integrity. The same openness to feelings, simplicity of speech, intimacy with the Father, spirit of humble service, compassionate healing, suffering discipleship, and obedient love is wrought in us by the Paraclete, accomplishing what Paul means by "new creation."

We ought to humbly underline the title "other Christs," for nothing less describes the reality. In days of yore, this dignity was reserved for an elite, a select few of the "holy nation" (1 Pet. 2:9) on the basis of ordination through the laying on of hands. Nothing is further from the gospel truth. This is a serious injustice to the "royal priesthood," which includes *all* the holy people of God. Every Christian who walks in the way of integrity and fidelity to the dream is "another Christ."

"No human beings are, by virtue of office or state in life, holier or more sacred in their persons or closer to God than others; and whatever sense we may now make of priesthood in the Christian community, we may never again think of priests and ministers as "other Christs" in a sense in which all Christian people cannot be called other Christs, nor can we see them as standing between God and others, mediators between God and humanity," states theologian James Mackey. "One is the mediator, Jesus, and through him all have immediate access to God. Neither cult nor creed, neither code nor institution, can ever again be allowed to rob people of the conviction conveyed in the mission of Jesus that God is Father to all, present to all in the gift of life and world which he gives to all without distinction, and accessible to all through the lives they live in the world they know."[5]

While the way of integrity offers no grounds for boasting because it is the work of the Spirit within us—and this is no token acknowledgment, for without the Holy Spirit we can't even see that Jesus is risen!—it does call each disciple to rigorous honesty about attitudes, values, lifestyle, and personal relationships. In my experience of life on the streets, honesty is a precious quality seldom found, and it is as rare in church as it is in society. Like the alcoholic who denies that he has a drinking problem, many of us have deluded ourselves for so long that dishonesty and self-deception have become an accepted way of life. The *esse quam videri* ("to be rather than seem to be") of St. Gregory Nazianzen has become so convoluted that "seeming to be" has become the common denominator of ordinary behavior, pretense and sham are enough to get by, pious thoughts replace putting on an apron and washing dirty feet, and in the words of Swiss psychologist Carl Jung, "neurosis is always an adequate substitute for suffering."[6]

In my broken days of sour wine and withered roses, when I was stashing vodka bottles in the bathroom, glove compartment, and geranium pot, I presumed that no one suspected and that the One who knows how to play Twenty Questions was having lunch in Nairobi. The mind plays tricks. Sober or inebriated, self-deception is a cunning, baffling, and powerful enemy of integrity. I have found no simple solution in the struggle for ruthless honesty, but (returning to the epitaph on my tombstone) I have begun to pause on the hour to briefly examine whether or not the thoughts, words, and deeds of the previous sixty minutes go with the flow of my dream of being a loving man. Should this practice lead to navel-gazing, unhealthy introversion, and self-preoccupation, I shall not ask how the jackass got into the ditch but simply work to get him out.

The gradual transformation from an attitude of self-hatred to a spirit of self-acceptance is what occurs in the process of trying to be honest. Paradoxically, the human spirit soars in the daily endeavor to make choices and decisions that are expressive of the truth of who we are in Christ Jesus, not who we think we should be or who somebody else wants us to be. Self-mastery over every form of sin, selfishness, emotional dishonesty, and degraded love is the less-traveled road to Christian freedom. "You cannot belong to Christ Jesus unless you crucify all self-indulgent desires and passions" (Gal. 5:24).

At the outset, the perfect joy of St. Francis may be an unrealistic expectation, but each small victory over self-indulgence yields its own measure of elation. The beginning of Brother Leo's peptic ulcer probably can be traced to the day that

Francis explained to him the meaning of perfect joy: "Above all the graces and gifts of the Holy Spirit which Christ gives to his friends is that of conquering himself and willingly enduring sufferings, insults, humiliations and hardships for the love of Christ." Leaving Brother Leo and levity in place, there is no growth without pain, no integrity without self-denial, and neither are particularly attractive apart from the personal love of Jesus Christ.

In the last analysis, the dream is not a way of thinking or a way of speaking but a way of *living*. Yet the way of integrity holds no real appeal to me independent of an intimate relationship with Jesus. Self-conquest for its own sake, penitential practices such as fasting and flagellation for self-discipline, and the spartan lifestyle as an end in itself are for souls braver than I. Unless Jesus enfleshes the dream and inspirits the integrity, discipleship loses its fascination and is stripped of its mystique. When the Crucified One says, "I'm dying to be with you," and then whispers, "Will you die a little to be with me?" my sluggish spirit is stirred (unfortunately not always) to prefer the pleasure of his company to whatever trinket of creation is mesmerizing me at the moment.

Thus the attitude of self-acceptance is not essentially self-centered. It is radically relational. It is not *self*-regarding but *Christ*-oriented. The spurious self-contentment that evolves from scrupulous self-examination, rigorous mortification, and the anxious endeavor to achieve purity of heart is bogus spirituality, the counterfeit coin of Christian integrity. As Jesus' unparalleled authenticity and inner serenity were rooted in his Father's good pleasure, so Christian self-acceptance is rooted in the conscious and experiential affirmation of Jesus in our struggle to be faithful.

A fellow Franciscan once challenged me with a set of questions:

> Do you ever reflect upon the fact that Jesus feels proud of you? Proud that you accepted the faith which he offered you? Proud that after he chose you, you chose him for a friend and Lord? Proud that you haven't given up? Proud that you believe in him enough to try again and again? Proud that you trust that he can help you? Do you ever think that Jesus appreciates you for wanting him, for wanting to say no to so many things that would separate you from him? Do you ever think that Jesus is grateful to you for pausing to smile and comfort one of his children who has a great need to see a smile, to feel a touch? Do you ever think of Jesus being grateful to you for learning more about him so that you can speak to others more deeply and truly about him? Do you ever think that Jesus can be angry or disappointed in you for not believing that he has forgiven you totally?
>
> Jesus said, "I do not call you servants, but friends. . . ." Therefore, there is the possibility of every feeling and emotion which can exist between friends to exist here and now between Jesus and you.

A wise man once said that a truly intelligent person is one who has learned to be happy with him/herself. The secret of self-acceptance, often hidden from the wise and clever, the

Ph.D.'s and powerbrokers of this world, is the way of integrity born of fidelity to the dream. If we are comfortable with ourselves, a newfound freedom blossoms. And so, the uncomfortable questions: "Am I free? If not, why not?" The familiar words of the Serenity Prayer—"God, grant me the serenity to accept the things I cannot change, the courage to change the things I can, and the wisdom to know the difference"— provoke the questions, "What is not working in my life? What am I afraid of losing? What is robbing me of inner peace? What attitude, behavioral pattern, or disordered relationship is making me frightened of the face in the mirror? Do I have the courage to change the things I can?" The mere willingness to confront the questions often unlocks the door to self-acceptance.

When we accept ourselves for what we are, we cease to hunger for power or the acceptance of others because our self-intimacy reinforces our sense of security. We are no longer preoccupied with being powerful or popular. We no longer fear criticism or contradiction because we accept the reality of human limitations: integrated, we are no longer plagued with the desire to please others because simply being true to ourselves brings lasting inner peace. We accept our feelings as part of ourselves. We appreciate and listen to them. Accepting our feelings allows us to choose appropriate behavior patterns that are beneficial to ourselves and others. Personality integration allows us to enjoy life responsibly and to discover the particular meaning of our own particular lives.

We are grateful for our lives and we deeply appreciate and love ourselves.[7]

The risk-taking disciple, who dares to listen to his feelings rather than to the pontifications of authority or the clamor of the majority, may quickly find that his inner convictions do not resonate with the *vox populi*. He finds the situation unnerving to himself and disturbing to the palace guard. Though Abraham Maslow might describe him as "unique and idiosyncratic, alive and creative rather than phony,"[8] the nervous disciple finds little solace in the eulogy. He is pretty damned frightened about swimming upstream—his security blanket of respectability has been snatched away, and he wanders temporarily in a Linus-like trance. His coveted image of propriety and sobriety, watchman against novelty and creativity, pillar of orthodoxy and vigilante of the *via media*, is blown to hell by innuendo, contrivances, and half-truths. "The crazy bastard wigged out," cries the bartender, and the sages on their stools nod gravely over their grog.

The risk-takers who listen to the Spirit speaking through "the intelligence of their emotions"[9] are ready to chance something, fully aware that the history of Christian spirituality is not consistently one of obedient conformity, however much some *savants* choose to view it that way. As Francis of Assisi, Martin Luther, Dietrich Bonhoeffer, and others saw, it is history of fidelity to the dream, writing the gospel afresh for one's own generation, and imaginative response to the needs of the church. Their dream, insofar as it comes from the passionate uncertainty of the Spirit, is contagious for some and delusional for the vociferous, lockstepping majority. The Scriptures testify that the innovator invites trouble. "It is better for one man to die for the people than for the whole people to die" (John 11:50). Heads shake, hallowed traditions are invoked, nonhistorical orthodoxy is extolled, and the guilt-tripping begins. Guilt-tripping is a cruel and powerful weapon, especially in the hands of professionals. It beclouds the issue at hand, destroys objectivity and turns discussion into diatribe. Retaliation is the predictable response of the immature and a potentially productive and creative conflict is defeated by mutual defensiveness.

Soon the risk-takers find that they are traveling in bad company. The historical Jesus was no outlaw, and nothing in the gospel lends support to the notion that he was a maverick harboring a grudge against the world, the law, or the authorities. Still, his family thought he needed custodial care (Mark 3:21), the Pharisees suspected a demonic seizure (Mark 3:22), and bystanders called him some very bad names. Jesus listened to another voice, sought his spiritual direction elsewhere, and seemed unafraid of what people might say about him or what people might do to him.

"Behaviorally, Jesus was perhaps judged unfaithful," notes therapist Kathleen Kelley. "He was at odds with the religious understandings faithfully held at the time; he broke laws and traditions when the love of persons demanded it. For Jesus it was more vital to be an honest, genuine human being than a model Jew. Fidelity for Jesus meant a total immersion in life to discover both his humanity and divinity."[10]

Begrudgingly, Jesus' enemies were forced to acknowledge his integrity: "We know that you are an honest man, that you are not afraid of anyone, because a man's rank means nothing to you, and that you teach the way of God in all honesty" (Mark 12:14). Though a ploy to trap him, this admission tells us something of the influence Jesus had on people. A life of integrity has prophetic clout, even among skeptics and unbelievers. Richard J. Foster has noted that the evangelical effect of the Methodist preacher John Wesley was tremendously enhanced by the integrity of his life. "Wesley is reported to have told his sister, 'Money never stays with me. It would burn me if it did. I throw it out of my hands as soon as possible, lest it should find its way within my heart.' He told everyone that, if at his death he had more than ten pounds (about $23) in his possession, people had the privilege of calling him a robber."[11]

Once upon a time in my seminary days, I was wrongly accused of insubordination and forewarned that not only would my future actions be monitored but my ordination was in jeopardy. It was a devastating moment. I was frightened and angry, filled with self-pity and confusion. The moment of truth and freedom came when I decided that ordination was not so almighty important—that it was more pleasing to God to be my real self than a model cleric, an honest disciple than an intimidated priest.

In the history of Christian discipleship, this little incident pales into insignificance beside the heroism of the apostles and martyrs; surely it will never be recorded in any anthology of the lives of the saints. Still, it gave me a taste for the way of integrity and a desire for the serenity of self-acceptance.

The imprisonment of eight members of the nonviolent Plowshares peace movement and the brutal murder of Salvadoran archbishop and peach activist Oscar Romero give us pause. They alert the Christian community to the dangers of discipleship and the price of integrity. Both assaulted tradition, unjust law, venal authorities, the past, and the establishment. The prophetic style points to the Cross. But it is the cross of Jesus Christ and only the cross that rises as a luminous signpost in the darkness of our world.

NOTES

1. James P. Mackey, *Jesus: The Man and the Myth* (New York: Paulist Press, 1979), p. 148.

2. Adrian van Kaam, *Looking for Jesus* (Denville, NJ: Dimension Books, 1978), p. 79.

3. Donald P. Gray, *Jesus: The Way to Freedom* (Winona, MN: St. Mary's College Press, 1972), p. 47. This little seventy-two-page book is scholarly yet eminently readable. It breathes the air of the gospel and suffuses the light of the Spirit. Gray's vision of Jesus is like refreshing rain falling on parched earth. I recommend it highly.

4. Gray, *Jesus: The Way to Freedom*, p. 50.

5. Mackey, *Jesus*, p. 265.

6. *Collected Works of C. G. Jung*, trans. R. F. C. Hull (Princeton, NJ: Princeton University Press, 1973). Quoted in Peck, *The Road Less Traveled* (New York: Simon & Schuster, 1978), p. 17.

7. Philomena Agudo, "Intimacy with the Self vs. Self-Alienation," in *Intimacy: Fifth Boston Psychotheological Symposium* (Whitinsville, MA: Affirmation Books, 1978), p. 18.

8. Abraham H. Maslow, *The Farther Reaches of Human Nature* (New York: Esalen Books, 1975). Quoted in ibid., p. 19.

9. See Martha Nussbaum, *Upheavals of Thought* (Cambridge, UK: Cambridge University Press, 2001), p. 38.

10. Kathleen E. Kelley, "Never Grow Tired of Doing What Is Right," in *Fidelity: Fifth Boston Psychotheological Symposium* (Whitinsville, MA: Affirmation Books, 1972), p. 122.

11. Richard J. Foster, *Freedom of Simplicity* (San Francisco: HarperSanFrancisco, 1981), p. 66.

7

COMPASSION AND
THE CROSS

BEVERLY HILLS, CA:—They call it the "Gold-Paved Gulch," the "Billion-Dollar Bazaar," the "Rolls Royce Raceway." In recent years Rodeo Drive, a scant three blocks of fashion and high finance, has eclipsed famous shopping streets the world over in status and flamboyant selling style. It is a gathering place for astronomically priced treasures and costly whimsies.

The shops boggle the imagination: the $43,000 blue-gray fox-fur bedspread, the $3,200 suede poncho to toss over jeans, the $125 haircut at John Peters's tonsorial parlor. Yet these astronomically priced whimsies are peanuts compared to the economic terrorism of the Enrons of the world. In a land of laws, the Enron CEO and his minions abandoned the law and business ethics in order to celebrate greed. Even as Enron collapsed, several Wall Street firms hyped the securities as good buys, and the accounting firm of Arthur Andersen issued "clean audits." Thousands of Enron employees, persuaded by unscrupulous managers to purchase more stock as the deck chairs of the sinking ship were being repainted, lost their life savings. In a corporate culture unimaginably defiled, the "know-nothing" defendants mocked a national tragedy and lined their pockets with untold millions of dollars through preemptive selling.

Elsewhere, the impoverishment and domestication of Christian faith is concretized when the acculturated Christ is associated with ruthless ambition, military ascendancy, financial success, and vindictiveness against marginal people; when politics is split off from faith, in order that issues such as war, weaponry, capital punishment, abortion, racism, poverty, and ecological havoc can be declared morally irrelevant and handed over to the peremptory apparatus of congressional committees and their brawny logic; when the prophets of fat living endorse cutbacks in federal assistance to the poor; when attitudes toward sex, money, and power are shaped by the prevailing ethos; and when the Word is deemed outdated.

"On many Sunday morning television presentations of Christianity," observes ethicist John Kavanaugh, "we hear much of money and success, often of psychological stability and social popularity, frequently of the glories of capitalism and the dangers of socialism, but rarely of the poor, the suffering, the rejected and disenfranchised."[1]

EL PASO, TX:—Directly across the border is the fifth-largest city in Mexico, Juarez, with a population of 750,000. Poverty of body, soul, and spirit ravages tens of thousands of these people in desperate want. The Lord's Food Bank was started here in 1975 by Rick Thomas to minister to the needy in the barrios and those who literally scavenge scraps from the city garbage dump.

A weary, sixty-eight-year-old woman named Juanita came for help. For years she had been rummaging through trash at the city market, barely managing to exist herself and attempting to feed her orphaned grand-children on whatever rotten food she could salvage from garbage cans. She was never able to retrieve enough for all the children to get something to eat. Sometimes they ate once a day; others, they would go without food for days at a time.

When the water shortage in Juarez became acute, people roamed the streets with buckets begging for something to drink. The temperature had been over 100 degrees for many days. Babies were dying of dehydra-tion. In the Food Bank area, families receive their water in 55-gallon drums from a passing truck if they have 20¢ to pay. During my visit it was shocking and heartbreak-ing to see people suffering the torture of thirst and babies dying for lack of water.

In any society, secular or sacred, where the haves don't share with the have-nots, the Kingdom of Satan reigns. The presence, the Word, and the dream of Jesus Christ are neither real nor operative. They simply do not exist.

We Americans make up only 5 percent of the world's popu-lation, but each year we consume almost half of the world's production of natural resources. While the poor in under-developed countries consider themselves fortunate to have shacks to shelter them from the weather, we enjoy compara-tively lavish luxuries—a summer home, a second automobile, a multicolored wardrobe. We eat grain-fed beef and annually throw to our pets enough food to feed large segments of the Third World. The population of Juarez could be fed off the garbage from our dumps.

Not being an economist, I have neither the academic background, scientific expertise, nor political savvy to spearhead a Christian revolution—or even to speak in an intelligent way to the urgent question of the redistribution of the world's resources. However, this much can be said without fear of contradiction or polemical exaggeration, that "the only sin of the rich man (Luke 16:19–31) seems to have been to live in luxury in the presence of dire need. If the sayings of Jesus do not imply that sharing one's wealth is a duty, they imply nothing."[2]

With the penury of the garbage dump and the luxury of Rodeo Drive in the background, we come to the theme of this final chapter: we relive the passion of Jesus through a life of compassion.

The etymology of the word *compassion* lies in two Latin words, *cum* and *patior*, meaning "to suffer with," to endure with, to struggle with, and to partake of the hunger, nakedness, loneliness, pain, and broken dreams of our brothers and sisters in the human family. Commitment to Jesus Christ without compassion for his people is a lie. "The life of Jesus suggests that godlikeness means to attain a compassionate life since God's heart is apparently thought by Jesus to be compassionate," argues Donald Gray. "To show compassion is to be like God, like Abba. To show compassion is to be like Abba's Son."[3]

To listen carefully to Jesus' words—"Be compassionate as your heavenly Father is compassionate" (Luke 6:36)—is to draw close to the Jesus of the gospels. Matthew's version reads, "You must therefore be perfect as your heavenly Father is perfect" (5:48). As was mentioned in Chapter 4, Scripture scholars tell us that the two words (*compassionate* and *perfect*) can be reduced to the same reality. Donald Senior asserts that "following Jesus in his ministry of compassion defines the meaning of being perfect as your heavenly Father is perfect."[4]

In the religious culture of first-century Palestine, the purity system of the Pharisees excluded sinners, the abject poor, lepers, the chronically ill, and so forth. Theologian Marcus Borg concludes that the clash between the inclusive vision of Jesus and the insular vision of the religious establishment ultimately led to Jesus' death. He writes,

> It is striking that "Be compassionate as God is compassionate" so closely echoes "Be holy as God is holy," even as it makes a radical substitution. The close parallel suggests that Jesus replaced the core value of purity with compassion. Compassion, not holiness, is the dominant quality of God, and is therefore to be the ethos of the community that mirrors God.[5]

The life of integrity born of fidelity to the dream has a precise meaning in the mind of Christ. It leaves no room for romanticized idealism, condescending pity, or sentimental piety. When a disciple's every response, word, and decision is motivated by compassion, he has "put on Christ" and walks in the way of integrity. Biblically, compassion means action. Copious Christian tears shed for the dehydrated babies in Juarez is heartfelt emotion; when combined with giving them a cup of water, it is compassion. The difference between emoting and acting is trenchantly described in the first letter of John: "If a man who was rich enough in this world's goods saw that one of his brothers was in need, but closed his heart to him, how could the love of God be living in him? My children, our love is not to be just words or mere talk, but something real and active" (1 John 3:18).

Every time the gospels mention that Jesus was moved with the deepest emotions or felt sorry for people, it led to his doing something—physical or inner healing, deliverance or exorcism, feeding the hungry crowds or intercessory prayer. The good Samaritan was commended precisely because he acted. The priest and Levite, paragons of Jewish virtue, flunked the test because they did not do anything. "Which of these three, in your opinion, was neighbor to the man who fell in with the robbers? The answer came, "the one who treated him with compassion." Jesus said to them, "Then go and do the same" (Luke 10:36–37).

The unglamorous and little-publicized works of mercy— feeding and sheltering, visiting the sick and incarcerated, educating, correcting, spreading healing words, bearing wrongs, counseling, washing dirty feet, and praying with people— embody the Kingdom lifestyle. So central is this teaching that at the final judgment God himself disappears and is recognizable only in human beings: "I tell you most solemnly, insofar as you did this to one of these least brothers of mine, you did it to me" (Matt. 25:40). "Thus it can be said with certitude that the Biblical meaning of spiritual perfection is to be compassionate," writes theologian Matthew Fox.[6]

Of course, the implication here is a very real death to self and to one's own invulnerable stands of rectitude, justice, fair play, and fun. Our natural repugnance and ingrained resistance to the inconvenient, unpleasant, and often messy business of compassionate caring is well illustrated by a story told at a recent AA meeting I attended:

A construction worker stopped after work for a few beers at the local watering hole and got home just in time for dinner. His little daughter, who had peanut butter and jelly all over her face, as well as a deposit in her pants, rushed into his arms. To say that he was "taken aback" would not accurately describe his emotional state. Wheeling around to his wife he muttered, "How the hell do you love something that smells like this?" Calmly she replied, "In the same way I love a husband who comes home stinking drunk and amorous. You *work* at it."

"Compassion is a spirituality of meat, not milk; of adults, not children; of love, not masochism; of justice, not philanthropy. It requires maturity, a big heart, a willingness to risk and imagination."[7]

Our human experience tells us that Christian marriage is usually not lived to a lyrical beat; it often comes to awkward expression in our fumbling attempts to forgive and make peace, to walk a mile in the other's moccasins, and to share the frightened, lonely, insecure, and sometimes neurotic journey of our spouse through the way of compassion. We can find echoes of ourselves in the petty, strange, and broken syllables of his or her story. With remarkable insight, seventeenth-century mystic Vincent DePaul wrote, "Be compassionate and you will become a saint."

However, in the contemporary church we have sufficient experience of failed human situations where continued cohabitation has become intolerable if not impossible. We must humbly acknowledge that, due to spiritual immaturity and inadequate preparation, many of the Christian marriages celebrated in the past have been neither *Christian* nor *celebrations*. The love of Christ for the church, actualized in every Christian marriage, is simply nonexistent when one or both spouses do not know Jesus. The crisis in the church is a crisis of faith—the need to know Jesus Christ as saving Lord—and married couples are knee-deep in the throes of the crisis.

The teaching of Jesus on the indissolubility of marriage is unbending and rigorous without qualification (Mark 10:1–12, Matt. 5:31–32, 19:3–12, and Luke 16:18). It must be assumed, then, that divorce is an evil and the cause of irreparable harm. Any attempt to mitigate the truth of this teaching would plunge the church into the moral morass of divorce on demand. Yet the absolute, total, and unequivocal prohibition of divorce often makes it impossible to show compassion.

The apostle to the nations did not hesitate to intervene in the case of a believer married to a nonbeliever. Invoking his own apostolic authority, Paul modified the teaching of Jesus and argued for the dissolution of certain marriages, because "God has called us to a life of peace" (1 Cor. 7:15). Thus did Paul interpret the teaching of Jesus on divorce a mere thirty years after the resurrection.

The church, the visible extension of Jesus Christ in time and space, is the image of the Compassionate One. Without diluting the gospel or abrogating tradition, we must not beg the question, "What would the Master do?" with a failed human situation that's unilaterally or mutually destructive and injurious to the lives of others. John McKenzie wrote,

> If the problem of divorce had been treated by the kind of reasoning which gave us the morality of legitimate self-defense and the just war, we should long ago have found the legitimate and just divorce. We have found ways to avoid the teaching of Jesus on violence which is as clear as his teaching on divorce. Apparently we see an "intrinsic evil" in sexual intercourse which we do not see in killing.[8]

Compassion is not sloppy sentimentality, nor does it compromise the truth. Clearly, the teaching of first-century Rabbi Hillel, which sanctioned a husband divorcing his wife because she was not a good cook, is lunatic liberalism. Any spirituality that tampers with the Word of God from naive humanitarian motives is bankrupt. St. Augustine observed long ago that, where there is any scent of a lie, the authority of the truth is immediately weakened. Biblical compassion, combining heartfelt emotion with active relief for the suffering, transcends psychological personalism and privatized pity to enter into the very heart and mystery of God. Clearminded, hardheaded, and softhearted, Jesus revealed in his ministry of mercy the face of the compassionate God.

Pursuing McKenzie's thought on divorce: "The Christian should be able to find a position between inhumane rigidity and amoral relaxation. Jesus certainly stated without qualification the principle that marriage is a stable and total commitment. Nothing is gained by viewing marriage as anything else. If it is a temporary sexual encounter it cannot be an element in a stable society. Jesus taught this: did he also teach that there is no recovery from mistakes, especially if they be the mistakes of others or the mistakes of adolescence? One needs clearer evidence than has been adduced that this is really the teaching of Jesus. There are irreparable sins and errors, like murder; one hopes that these can be kept to a minimum without encouraging them."[9]

The compassion of Jesus should motivate us to reexamine the personal response we make and the pastoral wisdom we proffer when confronted with a wedding invitation that does not fulfill all the manmade requirements for a "church marriage": it should further encourage us to assume the burden of moral responsibility for decisions and life situations which the Master did not prefabricate for us. An evangelical rule of thumb: Jesus seemed to have been less distressed by *faux pas* born of benevolence than by errors arising from legalism.

In the days before tawdry Times Square was gentrified into Disneyland, I took several vacation days in order to have a lengthy visit with the staff of Covenant House in New York City. That community residence is located on Eighth Avenue between Forty-third and Forty-fourth Streets. The community is tightly knit, the life of prayer real and rhythmic, the ministry to runaway children, teenage prostitutes, and chemically dependent youth exhausting and deeply evangelical.

Late one afternoon, during that New York visit, I sauntered down Eighth Avenue heading uptown. When I saw a muscle-bound pimp screaming filth at one of the girls in his stable, I continued walking. On the next street, the movie marquee blinked "kiddie porn" and cautioned the fainthearted not to venture inside. On a nearby corner, two Hispanic hookers in their mid-twenties were soliciting unwary customers. I retreated into a doorway and proceeded to pass through several shades of the emotional spectrum—from a wave of revolt and disgust to anger and frustration, then to sadness, emptiness, and pain.

The compassionate love of Jesus Christ is another matter entirely. His compassion surges from the bowels of his being, revealing a depth that defies human understanding and operating on a level that escapes human imitation. The numerous physical healings performed by Jesus to alleviate human misery only hint at the anguish in the heart of God's Son for suffering humanity. Here the disciple and the seeker after truth kneel in the presence of Mystery.

Albert Nolan writes,

The English word for "compassion" is far too weak to express the emotion that moved Jesus. The Greek verb *splagchnizomai* used in all these texts is derived from the noun *splagchnon*, which means intestines, bowels, entrails or heart, that is to say, the inward parts from which strong emotions seem to arise. The Greek verb therefore means a movement or impulse that wells up from one's very entrails, a gut reaction. That is why English translations have to resort to expressions like "he was *moved* with compassion or pity" (NIV, NRSV, JB) or he *felt* sorry (JB) or "his *heart* went out to them" (NEB). But even these do not capture the deep physical and emotional flavor of the Greek word for compassion. That Jesus was moved by some such emotion is beyond all reasonable doubt.[10]

The Christ who weeps over godforsaken neighborhoods such as the old Times Square is a man of sorrows moved in the pit of his stomach for the lostness of the sheep who do not know him. The heart of the crucified Lord of Glory does not turn away in revulsion or disgust at the wretchedness and perversity of the human condition. There is no crime so horrible or no sin so despicable that it was left at the foot of the cross. "He took our sickness away and carried our diseases for us" (Isa. 53:4). How is this possible?

Because Jesus is God.

Jesus is the incarnation of the compassion of the Father. Meister Eckhart, a thirteenth-century mystic, wrote, "You may call God love; you may call God goodness; but the best name for God is Compassion."[11] What do all the exalted names—Son of God, Second Person of the Blessed Trinity, Kyrios, Pantocrator, and other christological titles bestowed on Jesus by a later age—signify but that God was present in the Compassionate One in a unique, extravagant, and definitive way? Through meal-sharing, storytelling, miraculous healing, preaching, teaching, and a life of compassion that knew no frontiers, boundaries, or sectarian divisions, Jesus inaugurated in his person the reign of God. In Jesus' own conduct the new age dawned; the messianic era erupted into history. His present-day disciples' loving concern, nonjudgmental attitude, and compassionate care for their brothers and sisters is the visible form in which the reign of God is manifested today. What makes the Kingdom come is heartfelt compassion. It is the way that God's lordship takes.

The ministry of the church to the lost sheep of the underworld, to the deprived at the garbage dump, to the habitués of Rodeo Drive, and to the denizens of every affluent nook and impoverished cranny of the globe where the Compassionate One is unknown is not motivated by a desire for novelty. Rather, it is a compulsion of love: "If we do not commit ourselves with urgency to the task of evangelization, we are guilty of an inexcusable lack of compassion," cautions the Lausanne Committee for World Evangelization."

The church and the Bible are not substitutes for God; they are means through which we make conscious contact with Jesus Christ. They are the place of encounter with the Compassionate One, who reveals himself in sundry ways and diverse temperaments. The sinfulness and vulnerability of the disciples are no stumbling block, because "[his] power is at its best in weakness" (2 Cor. 12:9).

What is indeed crucial to the evangelical enterprise is the awareness that we ourselves are the primary target. It is not "they" who are poor, sinful, and lost. It is ourselves. Unless we acknowledge that we are the sinners, the sick ones, and the lost sheep for whom Jesus came, we do not belong to the "blessed" who know that they are poor and inherit the Kingdom. Enough of our pseudo-messianic posturing! Let us be done with our futile attempts to appear righteous before God! The Amen, the faithful, the true Witness says, "I know all about you: you are neither cold nor hot. I wish you were one or the other, but since you are neither, but only lukewarm, I will spit you out of my mouth. You say to yourself, 'I am rich, I have made a fortune, and have everything I want,' never realizing that you are wretchedly and pitiably poor, and blind and naked too" (Rev. 3:15–17).

In returning to ourselves, in contemplating the compassion of Jesus and realizing that "This means me," we come under the Mercy and qualify for the nametag "blessed." In urging us to compassionate caring for others, Jesus invites us to have compassion for ourselves. The measure of our compassion for others lies in proportion to our capacity for self-acceptance and self-affirmation. When the compassion of Christ is interiorized and appropriated to self, the breakthrough into being for others occurs. In a win-win situation, the way of compassionate caring for others brings healing to ourselves, and compassionate caring for ourselves brings healing to others. Solidarity with human suffering frees the one who receives and liberates the one who gives through the conscious awareness "I am the other."

Self-hatred stands as an insuperable obstacle to growth and maturity. It derails interaction with others and renders us impotent to give or receive love. The self-condemning memory selects only negative recollections. Previous kindnesses and thoughtful gestures are perceived as vitiated by self-seeking. All other emotions are blocked out, and a sense of personal worthlessness prevails. We become more closed, less communicative, less comfortable to be around. If prevailed upon to speak, we express deep disappointment at our lack of spiritual progress and dwell on the unlikelihood of future improvement. Caring for others is existentially impossible because we cannot be compassionate toward ourselves!

The thesis of this book is not gratuitous guesswork. Psychologists and psychiatrists, counselors and confessors live in the real world and devote an enormous amount of time and talent to people who dislike themselves. Years ago Carl Jung wrote,

The acceptance of oneself is the essence of the whole moral problem and the epitome of a whole outlook on life. That I feed the hungry, that I forgive an insult, that I love my enemy in the name of Christ—all these are undoubtedly great virtues. What I do unto the least of my brethren, that I do unto Christ. But what if I should discover that the least amongst them all, the poorest of all the beggars, the most impudent of all the offenders, the very enemy himself—that these are within me, and that I myself stand in need of the alms of my own kindness—that I myself am the enemy who must be loved—what then? As a rule, the Christian's attitude is then reversed; there is no longer any question of love or long-suffering; we say to the brother within us "Raca," and condemn and rage against ourselves. We hide it from the world; we refuse to admit ever having met this least among the lowly in ourselves.[13]

Who will rewrite the script for self-hatred? The Compassionate One! With a graciousness, a kindness, and an understanding of human weakness that only God could inhabit and exhibit, he liberates us from alienation and self-condemnation and offers a new possibility to each of us in our brokenness. He is the Savior who saves us from ourselves. His gospel is Good News indeed! Jesus, in effect, says, "Burn the old tapes spinning round in your head that bind you up and lock you into a self-centered stereotype. Listen to the new song of salvation written for those who know that they are poor. Let go of your fear of my Father and your dislike of yourself." The Knight of the Mirrors lied to Don Quixote when he told him,

> See yourself as you really are. Discover that you are not a noble knight, but an idiotic scarecrow of a man." And the Enchanter lies to you when he says, "Thou art no knight but a foolish pretender. Look in the mirror of reality. Behold things as they really are. What dost thou see? Naught but an aging fool." The Father of Lies twists the truth and distorts reality. He is the author of cynicism and skepticism, mistrust and despair, sick thinking and self-hatred. I am the Son of Compassion. You belong to me, and no one will tear you from my hand.[14]

Gray writes,

His compassion enables us to be compassionate toward ourselves. It is the divine compassion that Jesus embodies in human history and in his own compassionate life and death. Before I am asked to show compassion toward my brothers and sisters in their suffering, I am asked to accept the Father's compassion in my own life, to be transformed by it, to become caring and compassionate toward myself in my own suffering and hurt, in my own failure and need. The Father's loving graciousness is not in any way conditioned by or dependent upon what we are or do. He will be gracious and compassionate toward us no matter what we are or do. He will be gracious and compassionate toward us because that is the kind of Father he is—Abba. We should never speak of losing the state of grace in this sense, for God never stops being gracious and faithful to us. His being gracious does not depend on us—he will be unfailingly loving.[15]

We relive the passion of Jesus through a life of compassion. On the cross, the open arms of the Crucified reached out to feel the pain and suffering of the world. The Son of Compassion wanted to absorb the guilt, rejection, shame, and failure of his brothers and sisters. He came to us not with the crushing impact of unbearable glory but in the way of weakness, vulnerability, and need. Jesus was a naked, humiliated, exposed God on the cross who allowed us to get close to him.

Life teaches us how difficult it is to receive anything from someone who has all the answers, who is completely cool, utterly unafraid, invulnerable, needing nothing and no one, always on top of life and in control of every situation. We feel unnecessary, unneeded, and reluctant to receive. So Jesus comes in the way of weakness, giving us the chance to love him and making us feel that we have something to give him. Isaiah prophesied that the Messiah would be "like a lamb led to slaughter or a sheep before his shearers" (Isa. 53:7). Jesus, who understands the human heart, allowed the image of a dumb, helpless animal to be applied to himself.

The world does not understand vulnerability. Strength is made to look like weakness and freedom to look like failure. Vulnerability is flatly rejected by the world as incompetence, and compassionate caring is dismissed as unprofitable. The great deception of commercial television advertising is that being poor, vulnerable, and weak is uncool and ineffectual. For example, a fat monk named "Brother Dominic" is cute and cool because he buys into the competitive game of a copy machine. Social-climbing, power-plays, and winning breed a spirit of competition that bids farewell to compassion. The spirituality of the Servant is simply incomprehensible to the advertising industry. "The opening notes of Beethoven's Fifth Symphony are being employed to sell us pain reliever and the Prayer of St. Francis is being used to sell us hair conditioner."[16]

The cross of Jesus will ever remain a scandal and foolishness to discriminating disciples who seek a triumphal Savior and a prosperity gospel. Their number is legion. They are enemies of the cross of Christ. Jesus would have no other name by which he could be called were it not the name of the crucified. "He is unmistakable and identifiable only as the man of the cross."[17] His ministry was a seeming failure, his life appeared to have made no difference; he was a naked, murdered, ineffectual, losing God. But in that weakness and vulnerability, the world would come to know the love of the Abba of the Compassionate One.

Theologian Rosemary Haughton writes,

The paradox of passion is that the thrust of love seeking love consists in being vulnerable. . . . There is no dignity or shame in the naked suffering of the passion of Jesus. There is only utter vulnerability, a giving which is so absolute that Christian imagination has all too often been at work to mitigate the horror, either by supposing that the Son of God had evacuated the condemned body of Jesus at some point sufficiently beforehand to leave scope for majesty, or simply by sentimentalizing the thing into a kind of divine heroism. It is not heroism. It is simply love.[18]

The glory of Jesus lies in this: in weakness, vulnerability, and apparent failure he has called forth disciples to come after him, willing and able to carry the cross and relive his passion through a life of compassion. They are marginal people, not part of the scene, irrelevant to the "action." In their ministry of quiet presence they do not need to win or compete. The world ignores them. But they are building the Kingdom of God on earth by reaching out in vulnerability and weakness to share the suffering of their brothers and sisters. Where the Compassionate One is, there will his servants be. Whether in Times Square, Juarez, Rodeo Drive, middle-class suburbia, an alcoholic rehabilitation center, or a room full of eighth graders, the Word stands: "I assure you, as often as you did it for one of my least brothers or sisters, you did it for me."

The life of integrity finds its foundation and criterion in the cross, right down to the humdrum of everyday existence; and the passion of Jesus Christ is relived through compassion, right down to the nitty-gritty of everyday life.

NOTES

1. John Kavanaugh, *Following Christ in a Consumer Society* (Maryknoll, NY: Orbis Books, 1992), p. xiii.

2. John McKenzie, *What the Bible Says About the Problems of Contemporary Life* (Chicago: Thomas More Press, 1984), p. 252.

3. Donald P. Gray, *Jesus: The Way to Freedom* (Winona, MN: St. Mary's College Press, 1979), p. 70.

4. Donald Senior, C.P., *Jesus: A Gospel Portrait* (Cincinnati: Pflaum Standard, 1975), p. 105.

5. Marcus Borg, *Meeting Jesus Again for the First Time* (San Francisco: HarperSanFrancisco, 1994), pp. 53–54.

6. Matthew Fox, *A Spirituality Named Compassion and the Healing of the Global Village, Humpty Dumpty, and Us* (New York: HarperCollins Publishers, 1979), p. 32.

7. Fox, *A Spirituality Named Compassion and the Healing of the Global Village*, p. 17.

8. McKenzie, *What the Bible Says*, p. 157.

9. John McKenzie, "Jesus and Divorce," *Commonweal*, May 23, 1980, p. 305.

10. Albert Nolan, O.P., *Jesus Before Christianity* (Maryknoll, NY: Orbis Books, 1976), p. 28.

11. Source unknown.

12. "The Thailand Statement," *World Evangelization*, Information Bulletin no. 20 (a publication of the Lausanne Committee for World Evangelization), Sept. 1980, p. 6. Quoted in Richard J. Foster, *Freedom of Simplicity* (San Francisco: HarperSanFrancisco, 1981), p. 167.

13. C. G. Jung, *Modern Man in Search of a Soul* (New York: Harcourt, Brace & World, 1933), p. 235. Quoted in Gray, *Jesus: The Way to Freedom*, p. 41.

14. Miguel Cervantes, *Don Quixote de la Mancha,* multiple editions.

15. Gray, *Jesus: The Way to Freedom,* p. 41.

16. Fox, *A Spirituality Named Compassion,* p. 209.

17. Ernst Käsemann, *Perspectives on Paul* (Philadelphia: Fortress Press, 1971), p. 56.

18. Rosemary Haughton, *The Passionate God* (New York: Paulist Press, 1981), p. 149.

AFTERWORD

The challenge to grow old gracefully has lured me into a number of regrettable experiments. Seeking to draw attention to my senior status and to the deference I assumed was due to me, and further assuming that length of days automatically brought honor, I grew fitfully aware that I was being ignored. Thus I elected to become grumpy, persnickety, redundant, imperious, pedantic, rancorous, and finally a "Nobodaddy" (the "grandfather of nothing"), acidly satirized by poet William Blake. Not only was I denied the esteem I sought, but the *cognoscenti* soughed at the onset of my senility.

My next gambit was pumping iron and embarking on abdominal exercises, including strenuous sit-ups. Surely my family and friends would marvel at a senior citizen with bulging biceps, iron pecs, and a streamlined waistline! Alas, no. The reward for my herculean efforts was giggles.

Then logic rushed to my rescue. I reasoned that more knowledge would make me a more "interesting" person. After all, knowledge is power. So I speed-read poetry, biographies, psychology, comic strips, and dense theological tomes. I met with several "interesting" people who think money and talk weather, hoping to learn from them. To my surprise, when they were introduced to my multifaceted profundities, they were stung to the quick by my garrulous genius and retreated in shame. "Puzzling," I mused. The troubling thought of my vulgarity in seeking attention and admiration was quickly dismissed as a demonic ploy to savage my self-worth.

In desperation, I turned to a trusted friend. With a bemused expression, he recommended a bracing book, *Wisdom: The Feminine Face of God*, by octogenarian Daniel Berrigan. I was pleased to see that Berrigan wrote about this perplexing issue of aging gracefully, recommending "mindfulness, intelligence, discernment." Then he stated rather forcefully the importance of returning to the essentials of the Christian tradition: prayer, silence, solitude, sacrament, honesty, and community. And he added, "No matter one's sum of years: be steadfast."[1]

This undramatic program for growing old gracefully is the one I'm presently investigating. You see, the older I get, the more I ask myself, "How is my life unfolding in terms of its primary goal of living with God forever?" At the same time, I'm discovering how important transparency has become for an old fart in a cheap suit. And I'm wondering just how dangerous it is to choose not to love the life we're given.

So, as I slosh nimbly through the puddles of advancing age, it would be untimely and absolutely inappropriate for me to write mincing pastorals, sensitive soul-blubber, and well-behaved meditations for pious people. In this little book I've given my heart and my language license to be what they are:

crude and soft-spoken, whole and stricken, honest and provocative, drawn from the casks of life.

On the day that I began this manuscript a friend advised, "Write your book as if you were going to die the day it's published." A melodramatic flourish, no doubt; but in the waning sunlight of the winter solstice, I'm struck by the lateness of the hour, the paramount importance of truth-telling, and the urgency of personal integrity.

Within these pages is a glimpse of the Jesus of my life— dreamer and storyteller, parable of the Father, servant, friend, Savior, and stranger to self-hatred. He calls me back home to himself and myself. Jesus is God for me, not because of the exalted titles bestowed on him by later ages, but because he's the Compassionate One—compassionate not because he's Son of God but Son of God because he's compassionate in a way that eludes human comprehension and possibility.

Lastly, let me share one thing that I have learned during the forty-seven years of my ragged journey: if you call Jesus Goodness, he will be good to you; if you call him Love, he will be loving to you; but if you call him Compassion, he will know that you know.

NOTES

1. Daniel Berrigan, *Wisdom: The Feminine Face of God* (Chicago: Sheed & Ward, 2001), p. 65.